BORN IN THE USA

THE BOOK OF AMERICAN ORIGINS

D0370100

TREVOR HOMER

SKYHORSE PUBLISHING

Skyhorse Publishing books may be purchased in bulk at special discounts for sales promotion, corporate gifts, fund-raising, or educational purposes. Special editions can also be created to specifications. For details, contact the Special Sales Department, Skyhorse Publishing, 555 Eighth Avenue, Suite 903, New York, NY 10018 or info@skyhorsepublishing.com.

www.skyhorsepublishing.com

10 9 8 7 6 5 4 3 2 1

Library of Congress Cataloging-in-Publication Data

Homer, Trevor.

Born in the USA : the book of American origins / Trevor Homer.

p. cm.

Includes bibliographical references.

ISBN 978-1-60239-711-8 (alk. paper)

1. United States—Civilization—Miscellanea. 2. United States—Social life and customs—Miscellanea. 3.Material culture—United States—Miscellanea. 4.Popular culture—United States—Miscellanea.I. Title. II. Title: Born in the U.S.A.

E169.1.H7625 2008

973--dc22

2008046630

Printed in China

Contents

Acknowledgments

My thanks are due to the many hundreds of specialists who compile reference works, to David Haviland, who helped in my early endeavors, and to Ron Shuck for all his support.

I am particularly indebted to Alaina Sudeith, who edited my manuscript with skill and patience, and also to my literary agent, Andrew Lownie.

Sue, Max, and James—my family—this book is also for you.

BORN IN THE USA

Introduction

The United States of America has only been inhabited in significant numbers since the seventeenth century, and even today no more than five percent of the world's population lives within its borders. Yet the United States has spawned more new products, medicines, leisure pursuits, singers, writers, labor-saving devices, and businesses than any other country, ancient or modern.

More Nobel Prize winners in the fields of science and medicine have come from the United States than from any other country. The USA is unique among the nations in that the only human beings to have "slipped the surly bonds of Earth" and visited another planetary body were all Americans. At the time of writing, the only people to have traveled outside the orbit of the Earth were Americans—all born in the USA. No other country has even tried.

In short, America has been responsible for thousands of discoveries, innovations, and inventions, and this relentless pace of advancement only seems to be quickening. This book celebrates the work and achievements of the great pioneers at the very heart of the USA itself, but alongside the successes of its greatest citizens, we have also arrayed a few of its excesses.

There are several competing claims as to who was the first person actually born in the USA. Some say that in 1587, Virginia Dare, born to English parents, was the first. Others believe that Martin de Arguelles, born to Spanish parents in 1566, beat her to it. Still others claim the winner to be Snorri Thorfinnson, who was born to Icelandic parents in the year 1000.

Actually, sometime between 35,000 and 15,000 years ago, human beings crossed the land bridge between Asia and North America and journeyed south through what is now Canada into the present-day USA. Whatever the true date, there must have been a child born to those migrating Asians, and that child was the very first to be born in the USA—or the region that would one day become the USA, at least.

If any of those children could return to the present and see everything that has been born in the USA since their days, they would be awestruck.

From Bubble Wrap and bubblegum to burglar alarms and the Bill of Rights, from men-on-the-moon and Monopoly to microwave ovens and M&Ms, let's take a look at the things that would have filled those children with awe.

We will be no less awestruck ourselves.

Everyday Items

ELECTRICITY SUPPLY, ELECTRICAL APPLIANCES, AND THE HOME

In New York City in 1882, Thomas Alva Edison (1847–1931) switched on his Pearl Street generating plant and brought in the world's first reliable, low-priced, public electricity supply. He had fifty-nine customers in Lower Manhattan.

Edison's development of the power plant and the way in which he distributed electricity led to the electrification of streets, homes, offices, and factories and to industrialization on an unprecedented scale. Within twenty years, cities throughout much of the developed world had followed Edison's example, creating massive power plants to produce and distribute electricity to a mass market.

Edison, a prolific inventor with 1,093 patents to his name, is credited with being the first to apply teamwork to the matter of invention. He introduced the teamwork process at his Menlo Park, New Jersey head-quarters, and his team invented or developed many of the electrical appliances we see in everyday use today. We will see some of their work throughout this book.

> "We shall make electricity so cheap, only the rich will burn candles."
>
> **— Thomas Alva Edison**

LIGHTBULB

In 1879, Sir Joseph Swan (1828–1914) of the UK and Thomas Alva Edison (1847–1931) of the USA, simultaneously, on opposite sides of the Atlantic, invented one of the most important products of the late nineteenth century: the long-lasting electric incandescent light bulb.

Edison and Swan formed a joint company, Ediswan, to produce the lamps commercially in England, and Edison went on to found General Electric.

AIR-CONDITIONING

Without modern air-conditioning, tropical and subtropical parts of the world would be unbearable for most people, and even lethal for some.

A natural form of air-conditioning has been used in India for hundreds of years. Wet leaves are draped across the entrance to a building, and as air currents pass through the leaves into the building, water evaporating from the leaves cools the air. The same principle of exchanging cool air for hot air is used in the modern air conditioner, invented by New Yorker Willis Haviland Carrier (1876–1950) in 1902. At the time, Carrier was employed at a printing company that was experiencing problems with four-color printing. This was due to inconsistencies in the air quality. Carrier came up with the solution—the ancestor of the modern-day air conditioner. He received a patent in 1906.

In 1924, the world's first modern air-conditioning for human comfort (rather than for improving an industrial process) went on trial at the J. L. Hudson Department Store in Detroit, Michigan. The experiment was a great success, and since then almost all new buildings have been equipped with air-conditioning units using the original principle developed by Carrier.

RAZORS and SHAVING

Historians believe that men have been shaving since the Stone Age, as based on the presence of flint shaving tools that they believe arrived around 30,000 to 25,000 BCE. Since the cutting edge of flint becomes blunt very quickly, these razors were probably not long-lasting, making them the world's first disposable razors. Development of razors continued through the Neolithic Period (also known as the New Stone Age) (8000 BCE to 2000 BCE). Archaeologists unearthed a stone razor dated around 4000 BCE, and with the development of metalworking in about 3000 BCE came the first copper razors, specimens of which have been uncovered in Egypt and India.

World leaders such as Alexander the Great (356–323 BCE), Scipio Africanus (236–183 BCE) (the conqueror of Hannibal), and the Roman Emperor Hadrian (76–138 CE) set the trend of always appearing in public clean shaven. Lesser mortals, who had previously allowed facial hair to grow untrimmed, soon followed their examples. The evolution of the safety razor began with the Perrett razor, developed in France by Jean-Jacques Perrett in the late 1700s. In the Perrett razor, the blade was held in place by a wooden guard, in the same fashion as a joiner's plane.

In 1847, the English inventor William Henson developed the first razor with a blade perpendicular to the handle (like a hoe). However, it was in the USA that the greatest leap forward in men's shaving took place.

Safety Razor (And Others)

It has passed into American folklore that the safety razor was invented by one of the great American visionary businessmen, King Camp Gillette (1855–1932). It is certainly true that in 1904 he was granted patent #775,134, for a safety razor with disposable blades, but Gillette was beaten to the first actual safety razor by the brothers Frederick, Richard, and Otto Kampfe, who filed their U.S. patent in 1880. (The Kampfes's razor superseded the old "cutthroat" type razor by positioning the handle so that it sat at right angles to the blade, rather like a garden hoe. It also incorporated a skin guard on one side of the razor's edge. The blade of forged steel was removable, but it required frequent sharpening, in the same way as the cutthroat.)

In the early 1890s, King Gillette held down a job as a traveling salesman for the Baltimore Seal Company. In this capacity he managed to meet William Painter, the inventor of the Crown Cork bottle cap. Painter became important in the development of Gillette's thinking by convincing him that the most successful inventions were purchased again and again by satisfied customers, once the original purchase had worn out or been discarded.

Gillette made several unsuccessful attempts at inventing products, but in 1895 he finally came up with the idea of the cheap, disposable razor blade. In 1901, after many production setbacks, he met William Nickerson, a graduate from MIT who, despite the so-called experts assuring him that it was impossible, succeeded in producing steel of the right strength and thinness. It took two years of continuous experimenting, but Gillette and Nickerson managed to produce a double-edged blade. The new blade, which was too small to resharpen, was designed to be simply discarded once the edges had lost their sharpness, like the ancient flint blades of 30,000 years before.

Gillette began to sell his razors in 1903 and in that first year, total volume sales for the Gillette Safety Razor Company of Boston, Massachusetts came to only fifty-one razors and 168 blades. But by the end of World War I, just fifteen years later, 3.5 million Gillette Safety razors and 32 million Gillette blades had been issued to the U.S. armed forces alone, and the world of men's shaving had changed forever.

Windup Razor

In 1910 Willis S. Shockey was granted a patent for a windup razor, the forerunner of the electric razor.

Shockey's invention incorporated a windup spring mechanism that drove a flywheel. The flywheel then maintained consistent power to drive a set of reciprocating blades.

Electric Razor

Although a clumsy form of electric razor had been patented in 1900, the first commercial success came with an invention by U.S. Army Lieutenant Colonel Jacob Schick (1878–1937). Schick invented the world's first electric (dry-shave) razor in 1927, and began marketing it in 1929, although he did not patent it until 1931. The razor incorporated a small electric motor and oscillating blades.

And another thing . . .

Schick also invented the General Jacobs Boat, which had a very shallow draft and was useful for delivering troops quickly in the shallow waters of a beach landing, as well as the Magazine Repeating Razor, in which the blades were loaded into the razor in clips, similar to the way a magazine is loaded into a repeating rifle.

REFRIGERATOR

In ancient India, Egypt, Greece, and Rome, wealthy citizens made use of snow cellars, which were pits dug into the ground and filled with straw and wood. The wood and straw provided insulation against the heat outside, and ice transported from mountains could be stored for several months in this way.

The first domestic refrigerator was developed in 1834 by American inventor Jacob Perkins (1766–1849). In this machine, a manually activated pump converted the heat produced into a heat loss between two separate chambers. It was not a commercial success because it took an exceptionally long time to reduce temperature sufficiently to cool liquids and keep food fresh.

The first commercially successful domestic electric refrigerator came in late 1916 courtesy of the Kelvinator Company of Detroit (now owned by Electrolux). The first Kelvinator used the same basic cooling principle as modern fridges but had a much cooler name.

SAFETY PIN

The humble safety pin was the creation of Walter Hunt (1785–1869) of New York. Hunt's wife had complained about continually pricking her finger with straight pins—the only pins available at the time—and in 1849, Hunt decided to do something about it. He fashioned a piece of brass wire into the shape we are familiar with today, with a simple metal catch to shield the sharp end. He applied for and was granted a patent.

Unfortunately for Hunt, he was $15 in debt at the time to a friend. To pay off the debt, he sold his patent for just $400 to W. R. Grace & Company and watched as his invention went on to make a million dollars for others. Hunt was a prolific inventor who seemed to care little for the commercial value of his string of inventions.

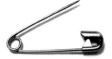

COAT HANGER

The wire coat hanger is one of those elegant and rare inventions that has managed to last a century with only minor refinements.

In 1903, Albert J. Parkhouse (1879–1927) was employed as an engineer by Timberlake and Sons in Jackson, Michigan, a company that specialized in wire novelties and lampshades. The story goes that Parkhouse returned to work after lunch one day and was unable to find a hook for his coat. Taking a piece of wire, he fashioned a rudimentary coat hanger with two loops to fit into the shoulders, and with the ends twisted together to form a hook. After some refinements, the lawyer for Timberlake and Sons, Charles L. Patterson, applied for a patent, naming *himself* as the inventor. The patent was granted and assigned to John Timberlake. (At the time, it was the general rule that all rights in an invention become the property of the inventor's employer.)

Although the product is still used throughout the world, and the company prospered enormously from producing the patented coat hangers, Albert Parkhouse never made a penny from his invention. He became embittered and left the company shortly afterward, moving his family from Michigan to Los Angeles, where he founded his own wire company. Albert died at only forty-eight from a ruptured ulcer.

SEWING MACHINE

As early as 1790, Thomas Saint obtained a British patent for a form of sewing machine. He neglected to build a working prototype, but a later machine, produced to his drawings, failed to work. The same thing happened in France in 1804, Germany in 1810, and Austria in 1814, with patents being issued for products that simply would not function. In 1818, John Adams Doge and John Knowles produced what was claimed at the time to be the first American sewing machine. This machine also failed to stand up to the rigor of actual work, although it did manage to sew a few stitches.

In 1834, Walter Hunt (1796–1859) of New York was the first to come up with the idea of a sewing machine in which the needles had the eye (hole) at the point. In a magnificent humanitarian gesture, Hunt decided not to patent his idea as he feared it would lead to mass unemployment if it resulted in the development of the automatic sewing machine. Elias Howe of Massachusetts had no such scruples, and patented an almost identical invention in 1845. He was to face years of patent litigation, but earned $2 million a year between 1854 and 1867 from patent royalties paid to him by other producers.

The first and most cumbersome sewing machines in the United States were produced in 1839 by Lerow and Blodgett Inc. The shuttle in the Lerow and Blodgett machine moved in a circle rather than reciprocating, as became popular in later designs. After repairing one of these machines, Isaac Merritt Singer (1811–1865) thought he had spotted a number of ways to improve its design. In 1851 he patented his own machine and formed I. M. Singer & Co., which went on to become the worldwide market leader.

What helped to make Singer's machines so popular, giving him a vital lead over the competition, was his pioneering hire-purchase system. This revolutionary idea allowed a customer to walk away with a sewing machine after a five-dollar down payment.

PHONES

Telephone

The telephone was invented in 1876 by Alexander Graham Bell (1847–1922) at the age of twenty-nine, though he had actually succeeded in transmitting speech sounds the year before. Elisha Gray (1835–1901) also claimed to have invented the telephone, but Bell beat him to the patent office by just a few hours, and a major court battle followed that went in favor of Bell.

Gray had produced a working prototype in 1874, but neglected to patent it because of interference by Samuel White, one of the investors in his company. White wanted Gray to focus on other inventions and saw little commercial value in the telephone. Although Gray's patent caveat had arrived at the patent office ahead of Bell's, he later withdrew it. The patent office allowed Bell to be named as the inventor.

Cell Phone

The use of a form of mobile telephone (two-way radio) was pioneered by the Chicago Police in the 1930s to stay ahead of Prohibition gangsters; "The Untouchables" led by Eliot Ness (1903–1957) were the first users. The technology behind these early models differs from that of the modern cell phone in that the receiving station did not pass from one cell to another, but had to remain within the broadcast area of the transmitting station.

The modern cellular phone was invented by Dr. Martin Cooper of Motorola, who first demonstrated the technology in 1973 in a call to his opposite number, Joel Engel, the head of research at the rival Bell Laboratories. For some years Motorola and Bell had gone head-to-head to be first with the new technology, but Cooper and Engel maintained their own friendly rivalry.

Hedy Lamarr (1914–2000), the 1930s Hollywood beauty, invented the frequency switching system that allows cell phones to communicate. The system works by rapidly switching the signal between the frequency channels. The changing frequencies are recognized by both the transmitter and receiver. Had she lived long enough and not lost the patent rights, which ran out before the cell phone had even been developed, Lamarr could have been one of the wealthiest women on earth. When the cell phone was finally launched, the companies were clear of patent liabilities.

TELEVISION

> "While theoretically and technically television may be feasible, commercially and financially it is an impossibility."
>
> **—Lee de Forest**
>
> (inventor of the Audion tube, and one of the "fathers of the electronic age")

Television, that staple of American life, has a mixed, international parentage, but the main developments came about in the 1920s with the privately funded work of Philo T. Farnsworth (1906–1971) in Los Angeles.

But before that, in 1884, the Prussian Paul Gottlieb Nipkow (1860–1940) claimed to have invented a means of transmitting pictures by wire, using rotating metal discs. The Nipkow Disc was perforated in a spiral pattern to divide the picture into a mosaic of points and lines. Although Nipkow was granted a patent at the Imperial Patent Office in Berlin, he was never able to demonstrate his system, and the patent lapsed for lack of interest.

In 1926, Britain's John Logie Baird (1888–1946) demonstrated a mechanical type of television that used a system of rotating discs similar to the Nipkow patent. Baird had successfully patented his invention in 1924, and the BBC adopted his system in 1929.

But Philo T. Farnsworth's wholly electronic American system replaced the Baird system in 1937. Farnsworth had produced the world's first working television system to use electronic scanning of both the pickup and display devices. At the time, his backers, a couple of local philanthropists, were pressing him to know when the invention would be paying them back some of their investment. To show that he understood what they wanted, the first image he displayed on the screen for his backers was a dollar sign. The first human image on Farnsworth's screen was of his wife. She was obliged to keep her eyes closed as his lighting was too intense to look at.

In 1928, Farnsworth demonstrated his system to the news media, and in 1934 to the general public.

And another thing . . .

Although Philo T. Farnsworth had been responsible for the most important developments in television, he only made a single appearance on screen. In 1957 he was the mystery guest on a popular quiz show *I've Got a Secret*.

Color Television

The first successful color television system was the brainchild of the Radio Corporation of America (RCA), which began broadcasting on December 17, 1953. The first program broadcast in color was an episode of *Dragnet*, a popular police series.

Television Commercial

On July 1, 1941 the Bulova Watch Company made history by broadcasting the world's first television commercial. The advertising spot for airtime on New York City NBC affiliate WNBT (now WNBC) cost just nine dollars. This meager sum secured a twenty-second slot immediately before a baseball game between the Brooklyn Dodgers and Philadelphia Phillies. The advertisement itself was fairly humble by modern standards. It consisted simply of an image of a map of the world, with a Bulova watch draped across as it, as the voice-over read the company slogan: "America runs on Bulova time."

ELECTRIC TOASTER

General Electric of the USA introduced what they claimed was the first electric toaster—invented by Frank Shailor—in 1909. A competing claim by Hotpoint puts their product launch date at 1905, but no evidence is available to confirm this claim.

VACUUM CLEANER

A British engineer named H. Cecil Booth created a forerunner of the vacuum cleaner in 1901. He developed a massive, gas-powered, horse-drawn cleaning device that he called Puffing Billy. The device was only used for commercial, not domestic, purposes. Booth would park it outside office buildings and shops and run a long hose inside for the cleaning operation. The dust and other detritus was collected outside, but unfortunately for Booth it was not a commercial success.

The domestic vacuum cleaner as we know it was invented in 1907 by James Spangler, a janitor in Ohio. The carpet sweeper he normally used was throwing dust into the air, and as this continuously troubled his asthma, he needed to trap the airborne particles. He concocted a device with a fan motor connected to a broom handle, which collected the dust in an old pillowcase. He was awarded a patent. Although modern designs bear very little relationship to Spangler's invention, the working principle is identical.

William Hoover (1849–1932), the husband of a customer of Spangler, liked the product so much he bought the company and rebranded the product line "Hoover." The name Hoover became the generic term for a vacuum cleaner, and hoovering became the verb to describe the action of vacuuming. The company went on to become a global brand.

VIAGRA

> "The only unnatural sexual behavior is none at all."
> **—Sigmund Freud** (1856–1939)

Men have sought aphrodisiacs and cures for erectile dysfunction from the time of ancient civilizations to the modern day. Everything from witches' brews to rigid penile inserts have been tried, with little reliable effect.

Finally, to massive worldwide acclaim (and relief), the drug Viagra became available in 1998 in the USA and a year later in Europe. Originally only available on a doctor's prescription, within three years of being launched, sales of Viagra had topped $1 billion annually worldwide.

Viagra (sildenafil citrate) was developed by the USA drug company Pfizer, initially as a treatment for angina. In clinical trials it failed to display any benefits to sufferers of angina but reports noted that it had the marked side effect of inducing strong sexual arousal in the male laboratory assistants.

Pfizer claims that, although there are only two names on the patent application, Peter Dunn and Albert Wood, there were literally hundreds of laboratory personnel involved in the development of the drug. One can imagine the enthusiasm to join the testing program. There simply was not enough room on the patent application form to fit all the names.

In America, Dr. Simon Campbell is regarded as the "father of Viagra," although he has stated he would rather be remembered as the father of Amlodipine, a cardiovascular drug.

LATEX CONDOM

In 1919, Frederick Killian of Ohio invented the process of hand-dipping natural latex rubber to produce condoms. The advantage of Killian's new process was that it made possible the production of very thin rubber sheaths that enhanced sensitivity during intercourse. Natural latex also retained its elasticity and had a long life on the retailer's shelf. Previously, condoms had been produced from "rubber cement," a form of liquid rubber that created a thick sheath, and aged quickly after drying.

By the mid-1930s, manufacturers were producing 1.5 million condoms every day for the American market.

TEDDY BEAR

The Teddy bear was named after Theodore Roosevelt (1858–1919), who was the twenty-sixth president of the United States and the first American to be awarded a Nobel Prize. Roosevelt was also distinguished for being the youngest man to become president, at only forty-two years old.

The Teddy bear "naming" came about during his first term in office when Roosevelt was out hunting game in Mississippi. It was a poor day, and his hosts were disappointed that the president's trip had been marred by a lack of sport. Members of the hunting party managed to chase a small bear cub up a tree, and invited Roosevelt, the guest of honor, to take the "trophy." He refused, stating that it simply would not be sporting to kill the trapped cub. Newspapers nationwide publicized the event, most notably the cartoonist Clifford Berryman (1869–1949) of the *Washington Post*, who used the headline DRAWING THE LINE IN MISSISSIPPI.

A New York shopkeeper named Morris Michtom read the story and came up with an idea. Michtom had several stuffed toy bears in his inventory, so he asked for the president's permission to dub them Teddy bears for marketing purposes. Roosevelt thought little of it, and, assuming that only a few would be sold under the scheme, he agreed without hesitation. However, the bears were a huge hit. Demand was so high that Michtom and his wife set up the Ideal Novelty and Toy Company, and within a few years, the name Teddy bear had become the worldwide generic term for toy bears.

> "If you could kick in the pants the person who is responsible for most of your troubles, you wouldn't sit down for a month."
> **—Theodore Roosevelt** (1856–1919)

WORK

BUBBLE WRAP

In 1957, two engineers named Alfred Fielding and Marc Chavannes created Bubble Wrap by accident in a garage in Hawthorne, New Jersey. They were actually trying to invent a new type of wallpaper. Their original idea was to produce textured plastic wallpaper with a paper backing, which could be cleaned easily. After they failed to achieve the effect they required, the product development followed an entirely different route. Bubble Wrap finally emerged from the wallpaper failure as one of the world's leading packaging materials.

Bubble Wrap's main commercial use is as a cushioned packaging material for fragile products or products sensitive to shock. However, it has also assumed a secondary use as a means of stress relief. After opening a package with Bubble Wrap in it, people noticed that popping the air-filled bubbles had a strangely pleasurable effect. In fact, Bubble Wrap is so effective at relieving stress that it is now widely used for the amusement and innocent distraction of children. There is even a virtual version of Bubble Wrap popping available on the company Web site.

And another thing . . .

There is an annual Bubble Wrap competition in which young inventors are encouraged to create a new product using Bubble Wrap. Prizes include a trip to New York and $10,000 in U.S. Savings Bonds. January 26 is celebrated as Bubble Wrap Appreciation Day.

HORSE-DRAWN REAPER

For thousands of years, crops were reaped by hand. Men and women toiled in the summer fields for days on end to cut wheat with only the aid of primitive hand tools like scythes and sickles. But in 1834, the agricultural revolution hit America like a tornado and hand reaping became a thing of the past.

While working on some of his father's earlier designs, which had proved unsuccessful, in 1831 Cyrus Hall McCormick Sr. (1809–1884) invented the horse-drawn reaper. He patented it in 1834. McCormick's reaper did as much work in a day as a gang of ten workmen could do in a week, making it the greatest agricultural advance since before biblical times.

As the newly laid railways opened up the West, so McCormick reapers were shipped farther and farther into farming communities that would have otherwise been forced to reap their crops by hand. Great farms were created, and the McCormick reaper was the only tool that could cope with the vast acreage of wheat.

William Henry Seward (1801–1872), who served as secretary of state to U.S. president Abraham Lincoln (1809–1865), said, "Thanks to the McCormick reaper, the line of civilization moves westward by thirty miles each year."

CASH REGISTER

The cash register was invented in 1879 by barman James Ritty (1837–1918) to keep an accurate check on cash transactions while he was away from the bar. The product proved popular, and interest in the registers was so strong that he decided to open a factory to produce them, calling his company the National Manufacturing Company. In 1884 Ritty sold the business to James Patterson for $6,500.

The company name changed to National Cash Register and it became a major international business. It was a forerunner of the early computer industry and in 1991 became a subsidiary of the massive American Telephone and Telegraph Corporation.

COMPUTER

Calculating machines have existed for more than 4,000 years, even pre-dating the invention of the abacus, but the modern electronic (digital) computer, probably the most important business and personal tool presently available, is strictly a creature of the modern era. The existence of the computer we know today has only been made possible by the continuous miniaturization of its component parts, and almost the whole of its development has taken place within a small area of the USA.

Digital computers work on the principle of binary code, using only 0 and 1 for all calculations, storage, retrieval, and instruction.

The modern computer came into being in 1939 when the Bulgarian American physicist John Vincent Atanasoff (1903–1995) built the first electronic digital computer. Atanasoff, whose father had emigrated from Bulgaria to the USA in 1889, hired Clifford Berry, a young electrical engineer, to help him, and they named their first machine the ABC (Atanasoff-Berry Computer).

Many of the subsequent developments in electronic computers were brought about by the work of an English scientist, Alan Turing (1912–1954) who worked in the secret code-breaking department at Bletchley Park, Buckinghamshire (a.k.a. Station X) during World War II. Turing designed the Turing/Welchman Bombe, an electromechanical device that was used to break the supposedly unbreakable German Enigma code. The American NCR Corporation went on to produce Bombes that operated much faster than their British counterparts.

The first fully automatic large-scale calculator/computer was built in 1944 by Howard Aiken (1900–1973) of the USA. It was known as the Harvard Mark I with more than 750,000 parts and was reputed to sound like a roomful of ladies knitting.

The first programmed electronic computer was built in 1946 by J. Presper Eckert (1919–1995) together with John W. Maunchly (1907–1980). It was named the ENIAC (Electronic Numerical Integrator and Calculator) and contained 20,000 vacuum tubes.

The first stored program computer was the EDVAC (Electronic Discrete Variable Automatic Computer). It was developed during the late 1940s and introduced in 1952. This followed the definitive paper on the subject entitled "The First Draft" written by Hungarian-born American mathematician Johnny von Neumann (1903–1957).

The semiconductor or integrated circuit was invented by Robert Noyce (1927–1990) of Fairchild Semiconductor and Jack Kilby (1923–2005) of Texas Instruments, who were working separately and without knowledge of the other's work. Kilby patented the discovery in 1958 and won the Nobel Prize for Physics in 2000. The invention stands as one of the most important of the twentieth century. Transistors, resistors, capacitors, and all the associated connecting wires were incorporated into a single miniaturized electronic circuit. The two companies shared information and helped to create a trillion-dollar industry.

> "What we didn't realize then was that the integrated circuit would reduce the cost of electronic functions by a factor of a million to one. Nothing had ever been done like that before."
>
> **—Jack Kilby**

Noyce went on to found Intel, the company that developed the computer microprocessor.

The computer microprocessor was invented in 1968 by U.S. engineer Marcian "Ted" Hoff (b. 1937). It is also called a microchip or chip. The chip places all the thinking parts of a computer, such as the central processing unit (CPU) and the memory, onto a single silicon chip. Hoff joined Intel as employee number 12 and his invention was first marketed in 1971 as the Intel 4004. Eighty percent of the world's computers now operate on Intel microchips.

And another thing . . .

In 1949 Edmund Berkeley (1909–1988) published plans to build SIMON in his book *Giant Brains, or Machines that Think*. SIMON was a desktop machine, about four cubic feet in size, that used relay technology, and some experts regard it as the forerunner of the personal computer.

POST-IT NOTE

In 1968, Spencer Silver was working as a scientist at 3M Corporation in the United States. He developed a reusable, pressure-sensitive adhesive, but couldn't find a practical use for it. He spent much of the next five years trying to promote his discovery within the company, but had no success.

One of Silver's colleagues, Art Fry, came up with the idea of using the adhesive to help bookmarks to stay in place. At the time of his "lightbulb moment" he was listening to a sermon in church and had become frustrated that the bookmarks in his hymnbook kept dropping to the floor.

Under 3M's "permitted bootlegging" policy, which allows employees to develop private uses for 3M products, Fry developed the idea of the Post-it Note. It was launched in 1977, but again was not a great success. After another year of frustration, 3M began a new marketing campaign by issuing free samples to residents in Boise, Idaho. The product immediately took off, and by 1980, Post-its were sold nationwide. A year later, the product was sold internationally in Europe and Canada.

AIRMAIL

The first transatlantic airmail link was established only six weeks after Charles Lindbergh made his historic first solo crossing of the Atlantic.

On June 29, 1927, U.S. airmen Richard E. Byrd, Bert Acosta, Bernt Balchen, and George Noville took off from Roosevelt Field, New York, to fly to France. The aircraft was a Fokker C-2. Thick fog in Paris forced them to change course and they had to ditch in the sea 275 meters (300 yards) off the beach at Ver-sur-Mer. The mail got damp but was still delivered.

The same beach became famous as Gold Beach in the D-day landings in Normandy.

Food

> "More die in the United States of too much food than of too little."
>
> **—J. K. Galbraith** (1908–2006)

GUM

Bubblegum

Frank Henry Fleer (d. 1921) developed a primitive type of bubblegum, which he blessed with the unappealing brand name of Blibber Blubber. It had the fatal flaw of turning brittle when blown into bubbles. It was hardly surprising that it failed miserably as a marketable product, and the company abandoned it after a single batch.

Enter Walter Diemer (1905–1998), an accountant employed by Fleer Corporation, who in 1928, managed to stumble on the formula for making bubblegum.

Although an accountant by training, Diemer was enough of an experimental food technologist to try different formulations, until he perfected the recipe for a gum that would stretch, but not stick to the face, when blown into a bubble. Despite all his intense experimental work to perfect the new product, Diemer always claimed that the final formula was just a lucky break.

After an initial trial batch sold out immediately, the Fleer Corporation went into full-scale production. Within the first year, sales of the new product, named Dubble Bubble, rose above $1.5 million. Fortunately for the Fleer Corporation, Diemer also turned out to be a natural salesman. He took charge of the sales force and personally taught them how to blow bubbles. He also instructed them on the best way to deliver effective sales demonstrations.

Diemer did not patent his invention, and thus received no royalties, but he stayed with Fleer Corporation until 1985, when he retired from the board at age eighty. He lived on until age ninety-three, perhaps testimony to the beneficial effect of blowing bubbles.

Chewing Gum

The ancient Greeks chewed mastic gum, which was a product of the mastic tree. Other ancient cultures in India and South America also enjoyed the benefits of chewing raw gum, which maintained dental hygiene before the toothbrush had been invented.

The first modern chewing gum was invented by Thomas Adams of New York in 1869 after a meeting with Antonio Lopez de Santa Anna (1794–1876), the exiled ex-president of Mexico. Santa Anna told him of chicle gum, which the native Mexicans had been chewing for years. Initially Adams tried to market a blend of chicle gum and rubber as a substitute material for carriage tires, but this failed. He then began selling a different formulation of a flavorless, but chewy, ball to be used as chewing gum, calling his product "chiclets."

And another thing . . .

The visible act of gum chewing, especially in Hollywood movies, has come to somehow symbolize certain character types: the tough, honest "prairie man;" the sparky, worldly wise teenager; and the stone-hearted gangster, among several others.

CHINESE FORTUNE COOKIE

The so-called Chinese fortune cookie is an American invention. They were not even eaten in China until 1990, when they were advertised as Genuine American Fortune Cookies.

Forty-niners, the Chinese laborers working in the California Gold Rush of 1849, first introduced fortune cookies. Not many Chinese prospectors made the big-time in the gold fields, and some turned to providing Chinese food to their compatriots. As more non-Chinese began to eat in Chinese restaurants, Chinese fortune cookies were introduced as an amusement at the end of a meal to the gullible locals.

COOKBOOK

The first American cookbook, written by an American for the American audience, was the delightfully titled, *American Cookery: Or, the Art of Dressing Viands, Fish, Poultry and Vegetables and the Best Modes of Making Pastes, Puffs, Pies, Tarts, Puddings, Custards and Preserves and All Kinds of Cakes from Imperial Plum to Plain Cake: Adapted to This Country and All Grades of Life.* The author was Amelia Simmons and it was published in Hartford, Connecticut in 1796.

American Cookery was a very important book. Michigan State University's Historical Cookbook Project stated that "the importance of this work cannot be overestimated." Its initial publication was, in its own way, a second Declaration of Independence. All the previous cookbooks available in the USA were only reprints of British publications, and had no information about how to use local ingredients. Simmons made generous use of indigenous American products such as corn, cranberries, squash, and turkey, which were not yet available in England, and importantly, she introduced to the American housewife the use of a chemical leavening agent, similar to modern baking powder.

Over the following thirty-five years, the book was reprinted several times. In 1808, Lucy Emerson plagiarized the New York edition, changing only the title from *American Cookery* to *New England Cookery.* The remainder of the book was copied verbatim.

CORN DOG (A.K.A. AMERICAN DOG)

The corn dog is very much an American dish—one that is almost unknown elsewhere.

It consists of a hot dog sausage, which is first coated in cornbread batter, then deep-fried in oil, or baked, and finally (in the case of the classic corn dog) served on a wooden stick.

The corn dog's precise origins are difficult to pin down, but in 1929 a Krusty Korn Dog Baker is mentioned in a book about kitchen collectibles, and in 1941 the *New York Times* ran an article referring to corn dog stands on Coney Island.

Some of today's commercial corn dog vendors claim to have invented the corn dog, but there is little firm evidence to support any of these claims. Carl and Neil Fletcher claim that "sometime" between 1938 and 1942, they introduced Corny Dogs at the Texas State Fair. Pronto Pup makes the same claim for the Minnesota State Fair of 1941. The owners of the Cozy Dog Drive-in of Springfield, Illinois, also reckon they were the first to serve corn dogs on a stick.

FROZEN FOOD

The practice of freezing food to preserve it can be traced back to the Chinese, who used ice cellars in about 1000 BCE, but commercial production of frozen food began in 1875 in America. Unfortunately, these early food-freezing methods suffered because the food froze too slowly. Slow freezing broke down the cell walls of the foodstuff, and failed to preserve texture, appearance, and most importantly, flavor.

In the 1920s, Clarence Birdseye (1886–1956) developed two methods for quick-freezing fish. While he was working as a fur trader in Canada, Birdseye had observed how the Inuit (Eskimo) people were able to preserve fish in preparation for the harsh Arctic winters by rapidly freezing it in seawater. He bought a simple electric fan and, using buckets of salt water and ice, devised an industrial method of flash-freezing food under pressure and packing it in waxed cardboard boxes. In 1924, Birdseye put his first frozen fish on sale, and founded an industry now worth $100 billion a year.

Starting with an initial investment of only $7.00 in 1924, with which he bought the fan and buckets, Birdseye sold out his patents in 1929 for $22 million. The product range was rebranded Birds Eye (two words) and is now famous worldwide.

HAMBURGER

The hamburger is an American icon, seen worldwide as the archetypal American food. Some of America's greatest fast-food chains—McDonald's, Wendy's, and Burger King—first popularized hamburgers, and by the closing years of the twentieth century had proliferated worldwide, with annual sales in the billions of dollars. McDonald's alone has 31,000 restaurants in more than 100 countries.

Many believe that German immigrants brought the hamburger to America during the early nineteenth century. After a slow start, its popularity grew, and during the first half of the twentieth century the hamburger grew in popularity to the extent that it became a staple American cooked food.

HOT DOG

The first recorded example of hot sausages being sold in bread rolls is of German New Yorker Charles Feltman (1841–1910) setting up a hot dog stand on Coney Island in 1870. Feltman first began to serve up the sausages in rolls because customers had started walking off with the white cloth gloves he had supplied to protect their fingers from the hot sausages. The association of hot dogs with baseball probably began in 1893 when the owner of the St. Louis Browns, a local brewer named Chris von der Ahe (1851–1913), began serving them at the stadium to accompany the beer from his brewery.

And another thing . . .

The first recorded mention of sausages is in Book 20, verse 25 of Homer's *Odyssey*, which was written around 850 BCE. In it he refers to a kind of blood sausage.

The term "fan" (as in "baseball fan" or "die-hard fan") is attributed to Chris von der Ahe, whose exaggerated German accent made it difficult for him to pronounce "fanatic" when describing the sort of people who watched baseball.

MICROWAVE OVEN

In early 1946, Dr. Percy Spencer (1894–1970) of Raytheon Corporation accidentally discovered the possibility of cooking by using "microwaves."

At the time of the discovery, he was doing experimental work with magnetrons, devices used for producing microwaves for use in radar. Spencer found that the chocolate bars in his jacket pocket mysteriously melted when he ran low-level microwaves. He filed a patent for the microwave oven in late 1946, and the first commercial oven went on the market in 1947.

The first domestic model was produced in the mid-1950s, priced at $1,295. As with all innovative technology, prices tumbled as volumes soared through the 1960s.

PIZZA

Pizza is a dish of Neapolitan origin, which in its home country has remained unchanged for centuries (other than for a few regional differences). The traditional *Pizza Margherita* is named after Margherita of Savoy (1851–1926), Queen Consort to the King of Italy, to commemorate her visit to Naples in 1889.

Innovations in pizza offerings, such as *Quatro Stagione* (Four Seasons—with four different toppings), *Vesuvio* (very hot and spicy, with lots of pepperoni), and the ubiquitous ham and pineapple, have almost all begun in the USA. This is also where the growth of pizza restaurants as a legitimate major food business came from, and the concept soon spread back into parts of Europe.

The first pizzeria in the USA belonged to Gennaro Lombardi in Spring Street, Manhattan, New York, in 1905 and it's still in operation today.

The creation of Chicago deep-dish pizza is jointly credited to Ike Sewell, a Texan businessman, and Ric Riccardo, who opened Pizzeria Uno in Chicago, serving their newly invented pizza in 1943.

POPSICLE

The Popsicle was created by one of the youngest inventors in history. In 1905, an eleven-year-old boy named Frank Epperson made a fruit-flavored drink, which he left out on his porch overnight, with a wooden stir stick left in the cup. Although Frank lived in California, the temperature dropped well below freezing that night. The next morning, he found the drink had frozen and the stick was firmly embedded.

He called it an Epsicle, but it was 1924 before he bothered to take out a patent, which he did only after the insistence of his children. He introduced the Popsicle to the public at Neptune Beach, Alameda, California.

Although it is a branded product, the word Popsicle has entered common parlance as the generic term for a frozen fruit juice lollipop.

CHOCOLATE CHIP COOKIE

The chocolate chip cookie is presently one of the most popular cookies being commercially produced in the United States. Its invention was an accident.

FOOD

In 1933, Ruth Wakefield, a professional cook and author of a cookbook, made the very first batch of chocolate chip cookies. There are two stories as to how this came to happen.

The Nestlé Company claims that Wakefield accidentally developed the recipe by adding small pieces of semisweet chocolate to a batter mix after she had run out of baker's chocolate. She thought the chocolate pieces would melt into the batter during the baking, but they remained in small chunks, and the cookies proved to be very popular. Later she sold the recipe to Nestlé in exchange for supplies of chocolate chips.

Contesting the Nestlé claim, Carol Cavanagh, who used to work for Wakefield, says Wakefield was an accomplished cook and would never have made such a simple mistake about melting chocolate. Cavanagh says that the addition of the chocolate pieces was accidental, resulting from a couple of bars of chocolate falling off a shelf into the batter mix where they broke up in the mixing. Wakefield was about to discard the batter when another member of the staff persuaded her to go ahead and cook it. Chocolate chip cookies were the result. According to Cavanagh, the recipe was not sold to Nestlé. Wakefield only gave them permission to print the recipe on some of their product packaging.

Whatever the true story, the chocolate chip cookie, which is as American as "Mom's apple pie," remains among the most popular cookies being produced anywhere.

POTATO CHIP

In 1853, an American restaurant owner and chef, George Crum, became an accidental inventor.

Crum invented potato chips after a visit by the railway and shipping magnate Cornelius Vanderbilt (1794–1877). Vanderbilt had complained loudly that the french fries served in Crum's New York restaurant were too thick. Crum was so angered by the remarks that he decided to teach Vanderbilt a lesson in manners and serve them up deep-fried and paper-thin. To his intense surprise, Vanderbilt was delighted with the new product and congratulated Crum on his innovation. After this, the new style of potato chips became a well-known delicacy, and Crum decided to call them Saratoga Chips.

Mass-marketing of potato chips began in the USA in 1926 when Mrs. Laura Scudder began to sell them in waxed paper bags. Mrs. Scudder invented the airtight bag, ironing together pieces of waxed paper to keep the chips fresh. Until that time, chips were distributed in large tins, which resulted in the last chips out of the tin usually being stale and broken into small pieces.

SLICED BREAD

Bread has been around since the Neolithic era (around 10000 BCE). The first known millstone, which was used to grind the grain into flour, is dated at around 7000 BCE.

In 1917, Otto Frederick Rohwedder of Davenport, Iowa, built his first prototype bread-slicing machine. It worked perfectly, but unfortunately for Rohwedder it was destroyed in a fire, and it took another eleven years before he had an effective replacement. The Chillicothe Baking Company of Chillicothe, Missouri, which used a Rohwedder machine from the start, and is still baking bread, claims to have been the first company in the world to market sliced bread. They began to market Kleen Maid Sliced Bread in 1928.

A competing, but unsupported, claim has been made by the city of Battle Creek that sliced bread was first sold there.

M&M

In 1940, Forrest Mars, Sr. (1904–1999) had the idea of producing a chocolate morsel covered with a hard candy coating. He had spotted soldiers in the Spanish Civil War eating a similar product, and when he returned to the USA he set about developing his new form of candy. In 1941 he was able to patent it.

During World War II, Mars restricted the supply of M&Ms to the U.S. military. The famous slogan, "The chocolate that melts in your mouth, not in your hand," was coined and trademarked in 1954.

SELF-SERVICE SHOPPING

In the first half of the twentieth century, retailers tended to staff their stores with a large number of assistants. Each assistant's task was to fetch goods for the customer, who generally stood waiting in front of a counter.

However, this practice is by its nature very labor-intensive, and as

The first Piggly Wiggly

staff wages increased, the idea of self-service developed. Self-service sped up the shopping process as, under the old system, the number of customers who could be served at any one time was limited to the number of assistants available.

Into this arena stepped Clarence Saunders (1881–1953), the flamboyant and innovative man who founded Piggly Wiggly stores. In 1916, Saunders opened his first self-service grocery store in Memphis, Tennessee, and patented his self-service procedures. The stores, which were the first to put prices on individual items, quickly became very popular. Saunders was able to franchise his ideas across several states.

As self-service developed, the practice of providing individually prewrapped grocery packages became prevalent, rendering obsolete the system in which employees had to measure out each customer's needs.

SUPERMARKET

According to some historians, the first true supermarket was opened in 1930 by Michael J. Cullen (1884–1936). Cullen set his store up in a 6,000-square-foot former garage in Queens, New York, and called it King Kullen. The company slogan was "Pile it high. Sell it low."

Grocery chains across America followed Cullen's lead by offering self-service in large buildings, and today it would be difficult to find a country without a supermarket.

Drink

BEER

Ancient people began brewing a form of beer at least 7,000 years ago, but in the USA, the "manufacture, transport, sale, import, export, delivery, and furnishing of beer" was actually made illegal for the whole of the 1920s and part of the 1930s—the period known round the world as Prohibition. The country has recovered very well after this enforced layoff, and hundreds of innovations in beer have been developed in the years since.

Toward the end of Prohibition, when Americans went to the polls to vote on reform, the great Will Rogers commented, "The South is dry and will vote dry. That is everyone sober enough to stagger to the polls."

Commercial Brewery

Tests on pottery jars from ancient Persia (present-day Iran) have revealed that they were used 7,000 years ago for holding beer. Archaeologists have even unearthed clay tablets from 4300 BCE containing a Babylonian recipe for producing the age-old beverage.

Ancient Romans drank beer from the fifth century BCE, and in the Middle Ages in England, it was used as a form of payment. You could even pay your taxes with beer!

But beer also has a distinguished history in America. The first American beer was brewed in 1587, on the Virginia estate of Sir Walter Raleigh (1552–1618). The colonists had been sending messages to England requesting better beer supplies, but after several failed promises, they lost patience and decided to brew their own. Despite the restrictions of Prohibition, beer has been brewed continuously in the USA ever since.

The first commercial brewery in America was founded in New Amsterdam (now New York) in 1612. By 1880, there were more than 2,000 breweries in the USA, but this number had dwindled by 1935 to just 160. The decline continued, and by 1992 most of the breweries had been consolidated into just five giant companies which controlled 90 percent of U.S. beer consumption. By 2003, the number had shrunk to only three companies: Anheuser-Busch (51%), Miller (19%), and Coors (11%), which controlled more than 80 percent of the whole market.

Changes in 1978 to the law of beer production led to the development of the craft breweries, which have now grown to number more than 1,400, and supply around 4 percent of the total beer consumed in the USA.

Steam Beer

Steam beer was the first type of beer to owe its origins entirely to the United States. It is highly effervescent, was first brewed in the 1880s in California, and is produced by brewing lager yeasts at the higher ale fermentation temperatures.

The first steam beer came about because of the lack of any refrigeration in the California of those years and almost no cold water. Brewers were forced to develop this innovative brewing process to meet the needs of the growing population of miners pouring into California during the Gold Rush and immediately afterward.

The unusual name (steam) may refer to the fact that the lack of refrigeration meant the beer had to be pumped to the brewery rooftop to cool in the Pacific breezes after brewing. The resultant cooling appeared from the ground to be a perpetual cloud of steam rising from the brewery.

Canned Beer

The world's first canned beer was brewed in America. The American Can Company had begun experimenting with canned beer in 1909, but found that beer reacted badly with the available metal. At the end of Prohibition in 1933, experiments were resumed and later that year a test batch of 2,000 cans was produced for public testing by Gottfried Krueger Brewing Company of Newark, New Jersey.

Feedback from the drinkers was enthusiastic, and Krueger Cream Ale, the world's first canned beer, was launched in 1935 in Richmond, Virginia. Ring-pulls had not been invented, so the cans had to be opened with a traditional can opener.

It was only six months before competitors, quick to spot a likely trend, broke into the canned beer market. Pabst was first, followed quickly by Schlitz.

The ring-pull (a.k.a. rimple) was introduced in 1963 by the Pittsburgh Brewing Company on their range of Iron City Beers. Ermal

Cleon Fraze of Dayton, Ohio had invented the ring-pull the year before and was awarded a patent early in 1963.

In 1975, Daniel F. Cudzik of Reynolds Metals in Richmond, Virginia, invented and patented a more environmentally friendly can opening system (the stay tab). By 1980, the stay tab had quietly joined the growing list of American world-dominant products by almost completely replacing the ring-pull.

TEA BAG

The tea bag was the accidental invention of a New York tea importer, Thomas Sullivan, in 1904. Sullivan had begun to send small samples of tea to his customers as a means of promoting his products, wrapping the samples in silk bags. Mistakenly, the customers started putting the entire bags into the pot to brew the tea rather than cutting them open as intended.

The tea bag was seen to save the chore of clearing away loose tea leaves and Sullivan was quick to seize the commercial opportunity that had landed in his lap. Thus the tea bag industry was born.

William Hermanson of Boston invented the special food-quality paper used in modern tea bags.

And another thing . . .

Tea is generally considered to be a British beverage, but it played a major part in the American Revolution. When the British parliament passed the Tea Act of 1773, which raised the level of tax, it precipitated the so-called Boston Tea Party, in which a full cargo of British tea was emptied into Boston Harbor in protest. As a demonstration of patriotism, the drinking of tea diminished rapidly throughout America, and coffee became established as the beverage of choice. It was only in the late twentieth century that tea began to make a comeback.

COCKTAIL

The unknown writer in an 1803 journal of agriculture, *The Farmers' Cabinet* (published in Amherst, Massachusetts), could hardly have imagined that a single word in his article would resonate through the years and come to be known around the world.

The article was the first known to have used the word "cocktail" in print. He wrote, "Drank a glass of cocktail—excellent for the head. Called at the Doct's. found Burnham—he looked very wise. Drank another cocktail."

The May 13, 1806, edition of the *Balance and Columbian Repository*, a weekly newspaper published in Hudson, New York, printed the first cocktail recipe. It read:

"Cocktail is a stimulating liquor composed of spirits of any kind, sugar, water, and bitters—it is vulgarly called a bittered sling and is supposed to be an excellent electioneering potion, inasmuch as it renders the heart stout and bold, at the same time that it fuddles the head. It is said, also to be of great use to a Democratic candidate: because a person, having swallowed a glass of it, is ready to swallow anything else."

So began the American love affair with the cocktail.

One of the earliest cocktails was the Sazerac, invented by Antoine Amedee Peychaude in New Orleans in 1850. The original recipe is hotly debated, but we do know that it was based on a combination of cognac and bitters such as Angostura. Later versions included the addition of rye whiskey or absinthe. It was another nine years before the Sazerac actually got its name, when a John Schiller chose the drink in honor of the opening of his new Sazerac Coffee House in New Orleans. The name is thought to have come from a popular brand of cognac of the time, Sazerac-du-Forge et Fils.

So popular did the drinking of cocktails become that by 1862 a professor Jerry Thomas had compiled a book of cocktail recipes. The book was called *How to Mix Drinks or The Bon Vivant's Companion*, and was primarily intended as a guide for bartenders. The guide also included recipes for punches, slings, cobblers, flips, sours, and toddies. Altogether the guide contained ten recipes for cocktails, which were distinguished from other drinks by the addition of bitters.

In May 1917, Mrs. Julius Walsh Jr. began a social trend by inviting fifty guests to a Sunday "cocktail party," which lasted for one hour and finished at 1:00 P.M.

BREATHALYZER

By the 1950s, the death toll on the world's roads was rising on a steep curve. Statistically, driving while under the influence of alcohol was causing one in six roadside deaths, and the race was on to devise an accurate means of detecting the amount a suspect driver had consumed.

In 1954, professor Robert Borkenstein (1913–2002) of Indiana University invented the breathalyzer. It works by measuring the amount of alcohol in a driver's breath when he or she breathes into a bag. The breathalyzer, which superseded the Drunkometer, uses infrared spectrophotometry.

HAPPY HOUR

Happy hour is used to promote discounted prices on alcoholic drinks during what is usually a slow time for business, such as between 4:00 P.M. and 7:00 P.M. Monday to Thursday.

In the early 1960s, happy hour entered the American way of life as a marketing term, and became a part of after-work life for all strata of the workforce.

The earliest recorded instance of happy hour is in 1920s America. The term "happy" was used to mean slightly drunk. As with many other clever American marketing techniques, happy hour percolated east and west across the Atlantic and Pacific Oceans and became a widely observed after-work ritual throughout the world. Concerns about drunk driving and the associated laws have curtailed its growth.

Clothing

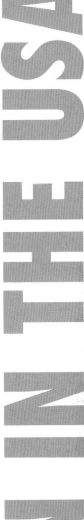

BRA or BRASSIERE

The word *brassiere* was first used in print in a 1907 edition of *Vogue*. The undergarment referred to was a form of large corset stiffened with whalebone inserts, which covered almost the whole body from the legs upward. The inserts were uncomfortable, and quite likely to put in an unwanted appearance in the décolletage. It was time for a change.

Women had been using a form of stiff fabric bra since Cretan times, but the first patented bra was invented in 1910 by New York socialite Mary Phelps Jacob (1891–1970). At the time, she was only nineteen and used the patent name of Caresse Crosby.

Her invention, which, unlike its predecessors, was soft and light-weight, and offered far more delicate support, was to become the standard undergarment for women all over the world. At the time, Phelps Jacob could not arouse much interest in her product, and sold the patent rights to Warner Brothers Corset Company, of Bridgeport, Connecticut for $1,500. Warner's went on to become the world's largest manufacturer of bras, and over the next thirty years they earned more than $15 million.

In 1935, Warner's introduced the cup size method of measuring women's breasts, and this is now standard throughout the world.

And another thing . . .

Mary Phelps Jacob also founded the Black Sun Press, which published the works of Ernest Hemingway, William Faulkner, Dorothy Parker, James Joyce, T. S. Eliot, Ezra Pound, and D. H. Lawrence.

BLOOMERS

In 1850, New Yorker Amelia Jenks Bloomer (1818–1894), who was an early women's rights campaigner and temperance advocate, designed what she called a "rational dress." Bloomer wrote a regular women's article for a New York newspaper and promoted a change of dress standards for women.

In one of the articles she wrote, "The costume of women should be suited to her wants and necessities. It should conduce at once to her health, comfort and usefulness; and while it should not fail also to conduce to her personal adornment, it should make that end of secondary importance."

The lower part of a pair of bloomers consisted of a form of Turkish trouser that was gathered at the ankle. The style was mocked at the time but briefly came back into fashion during the bicycle craze of the 1890s.

JEANS

The word "jeans," referring to the type of garment, is derived from a type of material that originated from Genoa in Italy. The word "denim," referring to the type of cloth, comes from *serge de Nimes.* (Serge is a type of cloth and Nimes is a town in France.)

In eighteenth-century America, as the cotton trade increased and plantation owners needed to provide their slaves with cheap but hard-wearing cloth, cotton replaced other materials such as serge in the manufacture of jeans. In 1848, after gold was found in California, the prospectors who flocked to the gold fields needed strong clothing that did not tear easily.

Enter Bavarian immigrant Leob (later Levi) Strauss (1829–1902). Strauss had left New York and crossed the continent to set up shop in San Francisco, planning to sell hard-wearing sailcloth to the miners. Strauss had the idea that the miners would use the cloth to make tents and shelters close to their mines. One fateful day a customer walked into Strauss's shop and advised him to make his cloth into pants for the miners.

Strauss took the plunge into garment production, and an industry was born.

In 1873, Levi Strauss & Company began using the pocket-stitch design. Strauss, together with David Jacobs (1831–1908), a tailor from Nevada, patented the process of putting copper rivets in jeans for strength. On May 20, 1873, they received their patent and this date was the "official birthday" of blue jeans.

Jeans have managed to remain fashionable for decades, albeit in a bewildering array of styles and designs. They were prominent in the cowboy movies of 1930s Hollywood, in which most of the actors wore jeans, and also symbolized the teenage rebel look of the 1950s. In the 1960s, the hippie movement favored jeans, and in the 1980s jeans even became high fashion, most notably in the Gloria Vanderbilt line of fashion clothing and accessories.

More than any other type of garment, jeans will always say "Born in the USA."

NYLON STOCKINGS

Nylon, the world's first entirely synthetic fiber, was developed in 1938 by Dr. Wallace Carothers (1896–1937). He made the discovery while conducting research into man-made polymers at E. I. Dupont de Nemours.

The first applications for nylon were in fishing lines and surgical sutures, but its most famous use was in the manufacture of hosiery stockings. Nylon stockings were first demonstrated to the public at the New York World's Fair of 1939, and went on to play a part in cementing Anglo-American relations. During World War II there was a massive shortage of all leisure and cosmetic products in Britain. As they were not yet available in British shops, nylon stockings quickly became the most popular gift the visiting American soldiers could offer their English girlfriends.

STETSON HAT

In 1860, John Stetson created a beaver-fur hat for himself while out panning for gold in Colorado. He made the hat with an abnormally large brim and a high crown. Looking outlandish for the time, it became something of a joke, but Stetson became fond of the hat and decided to keep it.

In 1865, he set up the John B. Stetson Company in St. Joseph, Missouri, using $100 of his savings, with the idea of manufacturing hats, and by 1885 his company had become the world's largest manufacturer of hats.

The company slogan is: "Stetson, it's not just a hat, it's *the* hat."

ZIPPER

Originally known as the slide fastener, the zipper offers a quicker and more effective fastening method than its predecessors: the hook and eye, the button and buttonhole, the clasp, the press stud, and a whole collection of pins, laces, and buckles.

In 1851, Elias Howe (1819–1967) had almost solved the problem of fastening garment apertures in one movement, when he was granted a patent for an Automatic, Continuous Clothing Closure. The invention did not possess a slider, but a series of clasps that slid along the edges of

the aperture, with each clasp securing the opposite edges of the garment. A string, which joined the clasps together, made sure the clasps were evenly spaced. The main difference between Howe's patent and the zipper is that the clasps were not permanently attached to the garment, but made themselves secure on the material.

And another thing . . .

Howe, who was an inveterate inventor, was the first American to be awarded a patent for an automatic sewing machine.

At the Chicago World Exposition of 1893, Whitcomb L. Judson (1836–1909) displayed the clasp locker, the forerunner of the zipper.

The clasp locker had an arrangement of hooks and eyes, with a clasp at the side for opening and closing them.

Judson's invention, however, had a serious drawback. It had the unfortunate habit of spontaneously springing open, and it was hardly surprising that garment and shoe manufacturers were reluctant to introduce the clasp locker fastening system, even as a fashion accessory.

One of Judson's engineers, a Swede named Gideon Sundback, was set the task of improving the clasp locker. In 1912, he produced the Hookless #2 fastening system, which substituted the hooks and eyes with spring clips. Thus was born the modern zipper.

In a strange turn of fate, Catharina Kuhn-Moos produced an almost identical device in the same year, in Europe.

The U.S. Navy, one of the earliest adopters, specified zip fasteners for pilots' flying suits in 1917.

And another thing . . .

In 1923, the B. F. Goodrich Company coined the term "zipper." According to legend, the company president himself provided the word. As he was addressing his development team he said, "What we need for this product is an action word—something that will dramatize the way the thing zips."

Science and

Technology

In the fields of science and technology, the United States of America rules supreme.

Nobel Prizes have appeared on the mantels of the leading American scientists since the early days of the award, and only the old Soviet Union has rivaled America for innovations in the space race. In the commercial application of technological advances, no other country is in sight.

Many scientific advances came from men such as Nikola Tesla, A. A. Michelson, and Albert Einstein—men who were born elsewhere but flourished in the freedom and the "can do" attitude they found in America. Their best works were born in the USA.

Here are some world-beating scientific advances to have come out of America.

BAR CODE

In 1932 a group of Harvard University students began research into a system to allow consumers to select products by removing punched cards from a catalog. When the punched cards were handed to a checker, they were fed into a scanner. The selected merchandise would be pulled from the storeroom automatically and delivered to the customer.

Many regard this as the initial concept behind the bar code, but the bar code we recognize today actually began in 1948. Bernard Silver (1924–1962) and Norman Woodland (b. 1921) were friends in Philadelphia and set about developing a system to read product information automatically at supermarket checkouts.

The idea came about while Silver was in college. He had overheard a conversation between the dean of students and a supermarket executive about having students work out how to capture product information at the checkout. He shared this information with Woodland, who was so keen to pursue the idea that he quit his job as a teacher to devote time to the project. Despite setbacks with instability in the ink they were trying to use, they filed a patent in 1949. Woodland figured that if Morse code could be used to send electronic messages, it should be possible to develop a system along those lines. One of their ideas was to have the bars in concentric rings in a bull's-eye pattern, but later they developed the straight-line system used today. Their patent was issued in 1952.

In 1962, Silver died at only thirty-eight, before his invention could be turned into a major commercial success.

The first UPC (Universal Product Code) scanner was installed in 1974 at Marsh's Supermarket in Troy, Ohio, and the first product scanned was a pack of Wrigley Juicy Fruit chewing gum.

A billion-dollar industry was born, and in 1992 Woodland was awarded the National Medal of Technology.

There have been claims that the ancient Irish script called OGHAM was a type of bar code, and there is a detectable similarity in the arrangement of symbols. However, students of bar codes, of which there are many, do not take these claims seriously.

COMPUTER MOUSE

The computer mouse is a pointing device that allows the user to direct a cursor on a computer screen and to issue instructions to the computer by means of "clicking" buttons. The mouse works by detecting two-dimensional movements relative to the surface it sits on, and uses that motion to direct the cursor.

In 1967, Dr. Douglas Engelbart (b. 1925) of the Stanford Research Institute, applied for a patent for the computer mouse. This was more than ten years before the personal computer was available to the public, and four years after he had invented it. The first device was made up of two wheels and a wooden shell, and Engelbart called it a mouse because the wire connection looked like a tail sticking out at the back.

The patent was granted to Engelbart in 1970, but no royalties were ever paid on it as his patent expired in 1987. He revealed in an interview that he had licensed the mouse to Apple Computers for a lump sum of $40,000.

Frustratingly for the inventor, this was before the personal computer made the mouse indispensable for inputting information.

DIGITAL WATCH

Digital watches display the time by means of a liquid crystal display rather than by moving "hands" as in conventional watches.

Nowadays it is a commonly used piece of technology, but when it was first introduced, during the years of the space race, it was considered to be the leader in the microelectronic consumer products revolution.

In 1957, the Hamilton Watch Company of Lancaster, Pennsylvania, produced the first electric watch, the Ventura. The Ventura retained the use of the balance wheel, and merely substituted the main spring with a battery. The need to wind the watch had been eliminated, but when the battery ran out, the watch simply stopped.

When it was introduced in 1961, the Bulova Accutron was the first watch to do away with the need for a spring. The Accutron used the oscillations of a tiny tuning fork to guarantee accuracy to within two seconds per day.

In 1972, HMW, the successor to the Hamilton Watch Company, bounced back with the Pulsar, the world's first true digital watch. By pushing a button at the side of the Pulsar, the time was displayed by liquid crystal numerals on a tiny screen. When it was first introduced, the price of the Pulsar came in at $2,100, which was roughly the price of a small car at the time.

As early as 1927, Bell Laboratories had produced the quartz clock. Warren Marrison (1896–1980) had demonstrated improved accuracy over conventional mechanical systems by using the constant vibrations of a quartz crystal when an electrical charge was passed through it. By the 1940s, time standard laboratories around the world were changing from mechanical clocks to quartz, but it would be another thirty years before electronic components had been reduced to a size that was suitable for watches.

E-MAIL

Instant messaging began with yodeling from the mountaintops and valleys, then arm-waving from farther away. Next it was smoke signals for even greater distances. More complicated messages could be passed by waving semaphore flags, and this was largely surpassed by the telegraph and then the telegram. Telex overtook telegrams and the fax machine overtook the telex.

The next important instant messaging format was the "electronic mail" (or "e-mail") system, which has now made almost all earlier forms obsolete. E-mail pre-dates the Internet and was an essential tool in its development. It is a form of "store and forward" communication that allows the sender to formulate a message and send it via computer. The receiver is able to access the message by downloading it from the e-mail server and reading it on his or her computer screen. The message can then be stored in the receiver's in-box, printed, or deleted. The effect is that computers are able to "talk" to each other.

Ray Tomlinson (b. 1941), the man who developed it, was the first person to send an e-mail. He did this in 1971 on the ARPAnet (see also Internet). Tomlinson's message was "qwertyuiop," the letters on the top line of a keyboard, and he chose the "@" symbol to denote which user was "at" which computer. Asked how he had come to invent such a thing as e-mail, when there was no known demand for it, Tomlinson said, "Because it seemed like a neat idea."

E-mail is now widely accepted in the business community as a low-cost means of communicating and synchronizing communications between people in different time zones.

E-mail, combined with the telephone, has taken over much of the need for face-to-face communication between people. Business and core social networks are frequently maintained through e-mail.

HUBBLE TELESCOPE

The Hubble Space Telescope allows far clearer observations to be taken than is possible with Earth-based telescopes. The Hubble telescope is named after American astronomer Edwin Hubble (1889–1953). It is the size of a school bus, and was carried into space on the NASA space shuttle in 1990. Several technical problems caused the original launch date of 1983 to be postponed, and it was not until the first servicing mission in 1993 that Hubble became fully operational.

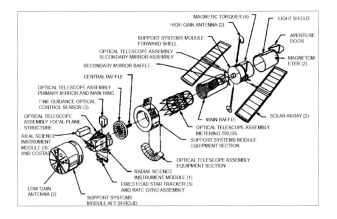

Edwin Hubble

Lyman Spitzer

The UK had launched an orbital solar telescope in 1962, with an expected life of one year, but Hubble is the only space telescope that can be serviced in space by astronauts.

The history of space telescopes can be traced back to a paper written by American physicist Lyman Spitzer (1914–1997) in 1946, titled, "Astronomical advantages of an extraterrestrial observatory." In the paper, he described in minute detail the advantages that a space telescope would have over a ground-based telescope. Spitzer, who is known as the "father of the space telescope," was also a key member of the team that developed sonar during World War II.

Even further back, in 1923, American, German, and Russian rocket engineers were speculating on how to send telescopes into space.

The advantages of having a telescope making observations in space (rather than from Earth), is that the images it produces are far sharper and not distorted by the Earth's atmosphere. The atmosphere is what causes stars to appear to "twinkle."

Hubble observations have led to major breakthroughs in astrophysics, and the rate of expansion of the known universe can now be accurately determined.

And another thing . . .

Interestingly, Hubble himself was better known for his athletic abilities as a young man rather than his scientific achievements. At one time he held the Illinois high-jump record.

THE INTERNET

The World Wide Web provides the facility for linking all the world's computers, making it easy to send documentation electronically via the Internet.

The forerunner of the Internet was the ARPANET. ARPA stands for Advanced Research Projects Agency, a division of the U.S. Department of Defense. ARPA, which possessed computers that were linked by dedicated telephone lines across North America, wanted them to be able to exchange information. ARPANET was planned in 1966, started working in 1969, and ceased operations in 1990.

The idea behind hypertext came from Vannevar Bush (1890–1974), a visionary engineer and science administrator. In 1945, when he was director of the Office of Scientific Research Committee and an adviser to U.S. president Harry Truman (1884–1972), he proposed the basics of hypertext with an idea he called "memex." Memex was a microfilm device on which to store records, books, and communication, and which could be accessed very rapidly. Bush even forecast that "new forms of encyclopedia will be born." Out of his ingenious concept of memex came the later development of hypertext.

LASER

The laser is only possible because of the way light interacts with electrons. Electrons can be "bumped" up to higher energy levels by stimulating them with light.

LASER is an acronym for Light Amplification by Stimulated Emission of Radiation, which means that laser devices produce intense beams of light of a very pure single color. The beam can be emitted at such a high intensity that it can vaporize the hardest of materials.

Lasers are used in bar-code readers, laser printers, optical storage devices, (DVD and CD), and in fiber-optic cable, which is essential in modern telecommunication. They are prominently used in surgical devices, replacing the scalpel and allowing microincisions that could otherwise not be attempted. In military applications such as range-finding and target illumination, the laser is an essential tool that is now so firmly established in everyday life it is sometimes difficult to remember that they were only invented within the last fifty years.

In 1917, Albert Einstein (1879–1955) recognized the existence of stimulated emission of light, but it was the 1950s before two Americans, Charles Townes (b. 1915) and Arthur Schawlow (1921–1999) were able to demonstrate the first device. The first working laser, based on a synthetic ruby crystal, was built in 1960 by the American physicist Theodore Maiman (1927–2007), working at Hughes Research Laboratories.

In the ruby laser, a ruby crystal is formed into a cylinder. A fully reflecting mirror is placed at one end and a partially reflecting mirror at the other. A high-intensity lamp is formed into a helix around the ruby cylinder. This provides the flash of white light that triggers the laser action. Blue and green wavelengths in the light excite electrons in chromium atoms to a higher energy level. The mirrors reflect some of this light back and forth inside the ruby crystal, stimulating other excited atoms to produce more red light, until the light pulse builds up to high power and drains the energy stored in the crystal.

Maiman obtained a patent for his invention, but after a thirty-year legal battle, part of the patent was awarded to Gordon Gould (1920–2005). Gould is credited with coining the word LASER in a paper presented in 1959.

PHOTOCOPIER

Known more accurately as xerography (literally "dry copy"), the process of photocopying was invented in 1937 by Seattle-born Chester Carlson (1906–1968). Photocopying is a complex process that, in simple terms, works by charging paper and powdered ink with opposite static electrical charges. Negatively charged ink is attracted to positively charged paper, and by applying heat to the whole product, the ink is fixed to the paper. The massive commercial potential was not realized until the 1950s when photocopying was exploited by the Haloid Corporation via their first product, the Xerox 915. Haloid was later renamed Xerox.

The first color copiers were developed in the 1970s.

RADIO

Nikola Tesla (1856–1943) was born in Serbia in 1856, moved to the USA in 1884, and was granted American citizenship in 1891. Working first with Thomas Edison and later with George Westinghouse, Tesla's major works in the field of electrical discoveries and inventions were achieved in America and his final count of patents exceeded 700.

Guglielmo Marconi (1874–1937) is widely regarded as the father of radio. By 1901 he had perfected a radio system, which was tested by transmitting Morse code across the Atlantic. But during the development of his radio, Marconi had in fact infringed seventeen patents previously registered by Nikola Tesla. Marconi's U.S. patent applications were initially turned down due to Tesla's previous work in 1893, but in a major turnaround, Marconi was granted a full patent for the invention of radio in 1904. Despite the award of the Nobel Prize for physics to Marconi in 1909, the patent for radio was reversed in favor of Tesla in 1943. Unfortunately for Tesla, it came a few months after his death.

The first voice broadcast on radio was a message sent from Brant Rock, Massachusetts, on Christmas Eve in 1906 to shipping in the Atlantic. The speaker, Reginald Fessenden (1866–1932) had previously transmitted from station to station (as opposed to broadcast) across the Potomac River in 1900.

The world's first commercial radio station was KDKA in Pittsburgh, USA, which began broadcasting in 1920.

SKYSCRAPER, ELEVATOR, and ESCALATOR

Two technological developments made higher buildings possible: improvements in steel technology that gave it greater tensile strength, and the development of safe passenger elevators in the USA.

Skyscraper

The first skyscraper was the ten-story Home Insurance Company building in Chicago built by Major William Le Baron Jenney in 1885 (see also "Architects," pg. 143). It was the first building to use steel-girder construction. The term skyscraper first came into use in the 1880s in the USA and was originally applied to buildings that were ten to twenty stories high. Nowadays the term is applied only to buildings above fifty stories high.

Elevator

The elevator was invented by Elisha Graves Otis (1811–1861). Otis had worked unsuccessfully in a number of different companies. During a break in his work, while he was trying to move redundant materials to the upper levels of an abandoned building (which he was trying to convert into a bedstead factory), he began to wonder how he could improve the safety aspects of hoisting platforms. At the time they were famously unreliable, and several accidents had occurred when hoisting cables had been severed. He came up with a spring-loaded device that would hold the platform secure if the hoisting cable was cut.

In 1853 at P.T. Barnum's Crystal Palace Exposition in New York, Otis conducted a dramatic public demonstration, using himself as the "guinea pig." While the elevator was aloft, with only Otis himself onboard, he arranged for a man with an axe to sever the hoisting rope. Without the safety device, the elevator car would have plunged to the ground. To the relief of the large crowd, he successfully showed that the elevator would only fall a few inches before the mechanism held it.

The first commercial passenger elevator had a steam-driven lifting mechanism, and was installed in 1857 at the E. V. Haugwout and Company Department Store in New York.

The Otis design was improved by fitting an electric motor to the underside of the elevator car, which pulled the elevator aloft by a cable. The first electric-powered elevator was installed for passenger use in Baltimore, Maryland, in 1887.

The Otis Elevator Company became the largest elevator company in the world.

Escalator

The forerunner of the modern escalator was invented in 1892 by Jesse W. Reno (1861–1947) and took the form of a large conveyor belt that was inclined at an angle of 25 degrees. It had a stationary handrail, which did not follow the belt round. The first example was installed in Coney Island, New York, in 1896.

The first escalator in the form of a moving staircase was produced and installed by the Otis Company at its own factory in 1899. Otis registered the word "escalator" as a trademark, but it quickly passed into common use and the registration was dropped. The world's first escalator installed for public use was at the Paris Exposition of 1900.

TEFLON

Teflon, which is also known as PTFE (Polytetrafluoroethylene), is the slippery surface coating seen on cooking utensils such as frying pans. It is used to prevent food from sticking to its container during the cooking process.

Teflon was discovered in 1938 in a lucky accident. Dr. Roy Plunkett (1910–1994) was working at the time in the research laboratories of the giant DuPont Chemical Company. On checking a compressed, frozen, 100-pound container of tetrafluoroethylene, he found a white powder possessing very unusual qualities had formed. The material had polymerized at low temperature into the product we know as Teflon.

In 1945, Teflon found its first important use during the Manhattan Project, when it was specified in the production of valves and seals for the world's first atom bomb.

The FDA (Food and Drug Administration) was reluctant to allow its use in cooking utensils until the 1950s when Tefal of France successfully launched a range of pans using Teflon.

Teflon-coated pans were shipped into the USA, where Teflon had originated, and were an immediate success.

There is an urban myth that Teflon was discovered during the Space Race of the 1960s. The rumor somehow spread that Teflon had been designed specifically for use as a coating on the tiles on the surface of the spacecraft, to prevent friction from causing the surface of the spacecraft to overheat on reentry. Teflon was used for this purpose, but was not specifically developed for the purpose. The EPA has now urged the manufacturers to cease production because of Teflon's containment properties.

BAKELITE

The Age of Plastics began with the invention of Bakelite.

Bakelite, which was first seen in 1907, was the first man-made thermoplastic material. When it was launched, its potential was quickly recognized and it became an immediate success; soon it was used in radio and telephone production. Later, it was discovered to have first-rate insulating properties and became the material of choice in the production of electrical insulators.

TELEGRAPH

The early telegraph was a machine for sending messages over long distances using electromagnetic current. Although the first electromagnetic telegraph was invented in 1837 by two English physicists, Sir Charles Wheatstone (1802–1875) and William Cooke (1806–1879), it was in America that the full national and international communication possibilities were realized.

Morse code was invented in 1838 (together with the Morse Telegraph) by Samuel Finley Breese Morse (1791–1872). On January 6, 1838, Morse succeeded in sending the first private, telegraphic message along a three-mile-long wire stretched around a room at the Speedwell Ironworks in New Jersey. The message read, A PATIENT WAITER IS NO LOSER. Morse developed a modified, simpler version of his code, known as International Morse Code, in 1851.

The first public telegraph line was erected in 1843 between Washington, D.C. and Baltimore—a distance of forty miles. Samuel

Morse sent the first message on May 24, 1844, over an experimental line. It said, "What hath God wrought?"

TELEGRAM

The first telegram, which printed letters and numbers instead of the dots and dashes of Morse code, was transmitted on April 8, 1851. A group of businessmen had formed the New York and Mississippi Valley Printing Telegraph Company, and the business started immediately with a license to use a printer invented by Royal E. House and 550 miles of wire.

Later the New York and Mississippi Valley Printing Telegraph Company changed its name to Western Union.

The first transatlantic cable for telegrams was laid in 1858 by Massachusetts-born Cyrus Field (1819–1892). It ran between Newfoundland and Ireland, and Queen Victoria (1819–1901) sent President Buchanan (1791–1868) a telegram of congratulations on its opening on August 16, 1858. After only a few weeks in use, the cable snapped in mid-ocean, but Field was up to the task. He managed to have each end dragged up the beach, and they were reconnected as a backup to a larger cable that he laid in 1866.

TRANSISTOR

There is a strong argument that the transistor, which is a device for amplifying or switching electronic signals, is the most important invention of the twentieth century. Its development allowed the replacement of fragile vacuum tubes with solid-state components, and led to the miniaturization of circuits in radio, television, and computer equipment. It also led to the development of the computer industry.

In 1947, William Shockley (1910–1989), working at Bell Laboratories, coinvented the point contact transistor, and later that year developed the junction transistor. For his work in this field Shockley and his coinventors, John Bardeen (1908–1991) and Walter Brattain (1902–1987), shared the 1956 Nobel Prize for physics, and Shockley is widely thought of as "the father of the electronic age."

The rise of that area south of San Francisco Bay in California known as Silicon Valley as the world's leading research and development center in electronics can be attributed to the invention of the transistor. Both Fairchild Semiconductor and Intel can trace their core businesses directly to the work of William Shockley.

Space and Space Travel

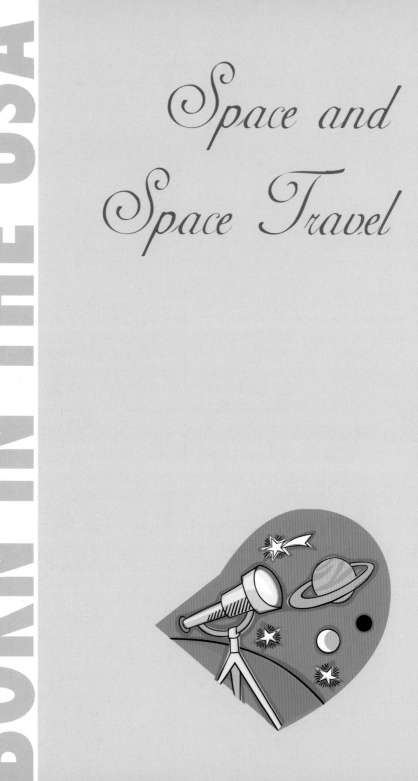

The massive efforts of the USA, through the National Aeronautics and Space Administration (NASA) have given it a clear international lead in the technology of space exploration and astronomy.

EXPANSION OF THE UNIVERSE

In 1920, after ten years of minute observation, the eminent American astronomer Edwin Hubble (1889–1953) was able to provide evidence of the expansion of the universe. He discovered during his observations of other galaxies that the degree of redshift (the visible light shifting toward the red end of the electromagnetic spectrum) increased in proportion to that galaxy's distance from the Milky Way. The light emitted by a galaxy starts at the blue end of the spectrum and it weakens and shifts toward the red end of the spectrum as the galaxy is farther away.

Hubble's Constant, which was written in 1929, is a law stating that the speed at which the galaxies are drifting apart is constant, and has stayed the same for between ten and twenty billion years.

RADIO ASTRONOMY

The birth of radio astronomy, which allows stars and galaxies to be studied at radio frequencies (audibly rather than visually), occurred accidentally in 1932. Twenty-seven-year-old U.S. radio engineer Karl Jansky (1905–1950) detected a source of cosmic static while he was investigating disturbances on the transatlantic telephone cable on behalf of his employer, Bell Telephone Laboratories. He attributed the interference to the interaction between ions and electrons in interstellar space and located the source of the interference as the center of our own galaxy, the Milky Way.

By the mid-1940s, astronomers were using large antennae to study faint radio sources from space and to obtain greater detail of the galaxies than was possible by optical observation.

RADAR ASTRONOMY

Radar astronomy is a technique for closely observing nearby astronomical objects by bouncing microwaves off them and analyzing their echoes. The technique is set to be a major help in Earth's defense against asteroid collision, as it is able to measure distances and changes of direction very accurately.

As early as 1946, astronomers in Hungary and the USA were able to bounce radar waves off the Moon and detect the reflected wave, and in 1958, radar waves were bounced off Venus for the first time.

Quasars

Quasars (quasi-stellar radio sources), are on the very edge of the observable universe, and are the brightest objects known. Allan Sandage (b. 1926) of Iowa City, Iowa, and Thomas Matthews discovered them in 1960 using radio astronomy.

Observation of quasars is now used for hyperaccurate measurement of time.

Black Holes

Black holes are collapsed stars that exert such strong gravitational pull, even light cannot escape them. Based only on human imagination, the unnamed theory of such entities had already existed for two centuries prior to the coining of the term "black hole," first used in a 1968 lecture given by American physicist John Wheeler (b. 1906).

In 1972, NASA's *Uhuru* X-ray satellite found the first evidence of a black hole in the binary star system Cygnus X-1. Cygnus X-1 is among the most studied astronomical objects and is estimated to have 8.7 times the mass of the Sun. It has been shown to be too dense to be anything other than a black hole.

And another thing . . .

American physicist Kip Thorne (b. 1940) won a scientific bet with Stephen Hawking as to whether Cygnus X-1 was a black hole. Hawking bet against it, and conceded the bet in 2004.

Pictures from Mars

The first pictures from the surface of Mars were beamed back to Earth on July 20, 1976, by the American space vehicle *Viking 1*, which had landed on Mars's surface. Transmission began only twenty-five seconds after the landing and took about four minutes.

For the next almost six and a half years, *Viking 1* transmitted more than 1,400 images back to Earth and would have sent many more but it ceased working in November 1982 after a human error during a software update. Along with its sister craft (*Viking 2*) it gathered samples for onboard biological analysis. The dual mission was to seek out evidence of life, and although early results looked promising, there is no clear-cut evidence. The results are still being assessed.

Mapping Venus

Venus was mapped for the first time in September 1994 by the U.S. space probe *Magellan*. The spacecraft had gone into orbit around Venus in 1990 and for four years it used radar imaging techniques to create near-photographic details of the planet's surface. After completion of its mission, *Magellan* was allowed to sink into the dense Venusian atmosphere. It is thought that it only partly vaporized, with some parts of the probe actually managing to hit the surface.

ROCKET SCIENCE

Solid-fuel rockets, which began in ninth-century China as no more than fireworks for the amusement of children, were eventually developed for use as missiles in war, and ultimately as vehicles to transport men and machinery into space.

The basic equations of rocketry were first calculated by the Russian physicist Konstantin Tsiolkovsky (1857–1935), who completed his work in 1903. He calculated that the required escape velocity from the Earth's gravitational pull for a space vehicle to enter orbit was eight kilometers per second. He also stated that to achieve the escape velocity would require a multistage rocket, so that once the fuel contained in a particular stage has been exhausted, the casing could be discarded. He speculated that the rocket should be fueled by liquid oxygen and liquid hydrogen, although other propellants have been developed since Tsiolkovsky's time. In his honor, the basic equation for rocket propulsion is known as the "Tsiolkovsky rocket equation."

Modern rocketry owes more to the secret work of Robert Goddard (1882–1945) in the early years of the twentieth century. Beginning in 1912, Goddard analyzed the requirements of practical rockets and developed both the multistage rocket concept and the use of the hourglass-shaped De Laval nozzle, which accelerates gas to supersonic speed. Most important, and despite ridicule in the press, Goddard proved mathematically that a rocket would work in a vacuum.

Liquid-Powered Rocket

The first liquid-powered rocket was produced in 1926 by Robert Goddard in Massachusetts. Goddard's first rocket rose to a height of just forty-one feet and managed to travel only 184 feet forward. The important result was that he had proved that his concept of liquid-powered rocket propulsion would work. For the fuel, Goddard used gasoline and oxygen mixed from separate tanks in the combustion chamber. The immense noise created by his rocket experiments resulted in serious complaints from the neighbors. In order to continue his work, Goddard was forced to move to the remote town of Roswell, New Mexico.

The U.S. Army failed to grasp the importance of rockets for war purposes, but the head of Nazi rocket development, Werner von Braun (1912–1977) adopted many of Goddard's plans in his V1 and V2 rocket designs. These were used to devastating effect against London during World War II.

Going to the Moon

Once humankind had mastered the science of rocketry, going to the Moon became a real possibility. Stimulated by their competing interests during the Cold War, and with each country desperate to prove its own superiority, the USA and the Soviet Union poured massive financial and scientific resources into the pursuit of space travel. Going to the Moon was the ultimate goal.

It was important that any men going to the Moon were able to rely on a "soft" landing and not crash into the lunar surface. Before men themselves were sent, both sides conducted soft-landing experiments, which were remote-controlled from the Earth. The USA's first unmanned soft landing on the Moon was made on June 2, 1966, by *Surveyor 1*. In February 1966, the USSR had managed to soft-land *Luna-9*, an unmanned vehicle, on the Moon. Widespread panic gripped NASA, as they had to face the unpalatable fact that they might yet be beaten to landing men on the Moon and bringing them back alive.

The Dark Side

The first manned spacecraft to travel to any celestial body was *Apollo 8* in 1968, and the crew members (Frank Borman, James Lovell, and William Anders) were the first humans to ever leave Earth's orbit. They went on to orbit the Moon and to fly past the dark side as, on Christmas Eve 1968, with the world holding its breath, they disappeared behind the Moon. This was the first time any human being had been out of view of (and out of any sort of contact with) the Earth. There were some very tense people in Ground Control back in Houston.

Sixty-eight hours and fifty-eight minutes into the flight, the spacecraft passed behind the rim of the Moon to the dark side. The dark-side journey was planned to last a total of ten minutes. To put the space capsule into circumlunar orbit, the crew had to fire the engine in a controlled burn while out of radio contact. There was no backup crew if anything went wrong, and any mistake in timing meant they could

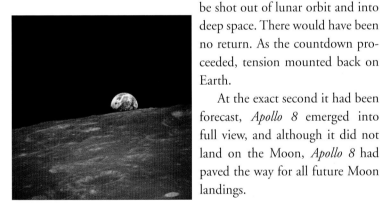

be shot out of lunar orbit and into deep space. There would have been no return. As the countdown proceeded, tension mounted back on Earth.

At the exact second it had been forecast, *Apollo 8* emerged into full view, and although it did not land on the Moon, *Apollo 8* had paved the way for all future Moon landings.

The first Earth rise photographed by humans

And another thing . . .

On the eve of their historic journey, the crew was visited by the most famous aviator in the world, Charles Lindbergh (1902–1974), who told them that he had used a piece of string stretched across a globe of the world to work out how much fuel he would need on his historic first solo flight across the Atlantic. He was interested to learn that *Apollo 8* burned more fuel in one tenth of every second than he had burned during his whole flight.

First Man on the Moon

On July 15, 1969, Neil Armstrong (b. 1930), became the first man to set foot on the Moon.

The objective of *Apollo 11* was to land safely rather than in a precise location, but the crew (Armstrong and Aldrin) noticed that landmarks on the Moon's surface were passing about two seconds too early. This would have forced them to land several miles beyond the landing zone. Armstrong took over manual control of the landing vehicle and touched down with only a few seconds of fuel left. The two crew members reached across to each other and just shook hands.

Armstrong had again demonstrated his coolness under duress. He had had a very close brush with death in December the previous year, when, with only a few seconds to spare, he managed to eject from a crashing Lunar Landing Vehicle for which he was the test pilot.

The first word ever spoken from the Moon to Earth was "Houston," as in "Houston, Tranquility Bay here. The Eagle has landed." Most people can remember Armstrong's words as he stepped from the ladder to the Moon's surface: "That's one small step for [a] man, one giant leap for mankind."

(The first word actually spoken on the Moon, but not for transmission to Earth, was "Contact" as in "Contact light" spoken by Edwin "Buzz" Aldrin [b. 1930] to Neil Armstrong.)

In a touching gesture of peace between nations, the *Apollo 11* crew left a memorial on the surface of the Moon to commemorate the lives of three deceased American astronauts, Gus Grissom, Ed White, and Roger Chaffee, alongside the names of two deceased Soviet cosmonauts, Yuri Gagarin and Vladimir Komarov.

And another thing . . .

The last word spoken from the surface of the Moon was "here" as in, "OK, let's get this mother out of here." The speaker was Gene Cernan, as the last Earth-bound spacecraft prepared to leave the surface of the Moon in December 1972.

CONSPIRACIES AND MYTHS

Moonmen

In 1835, the *New York Sun* published a lead story claiming that a new, powerful telescope had managed to focus on small objects on the surface of the Moon. The story claimed that astronomers had seen strange creatures (half bat, half man) flitting across the landscape. In the face of universal ridicule, the *New York Sun* was forced to issue a retraction.

No One Has Ever Been to the Moon

A 1995 poll by *Time* magazine revealed that 6 percent of Americans do not believe men ever went to the Moon. A Fox TV program broadcast on February 23, 2001, proposed the theory that the whole of the Moon landing program had been filmed in a studio. This conspiracy theory was based on such matters as the contrasting directions of shadows and the fact that the American flag appeared to be waving in a breeze. Each claim has largely been discredited, although there has been a surprising lack of response from NASA.

Urban Myths

After Neil Armstrong stepped onto the Moon's surface, he is supposed to have said, "Good luck, Mr. Gorski." This refers to a supposed incident during Armstrong's childhood, when he overheard his next-door neighbor Mrs. Gorski shouting at her husband, "You want oral sex? You'll get oral sex when the kid next door walks on the moon." Armstrong himself has never commented on this, and the story is largely discredited.

Michael Collins (b. 1930) was the pilot of the command module *Columbia* that remained in lunar orbit while Armstrong and Aldrin descended to the Moon's surface. On the journey from Earth, the crew had debated what Armstrong should say as he stepped from the lunar landing vehicle. Collins is supposed to have said, "If you'd got any balls, Neil, you'd say, 'Oh my God, what is that thing?' Then scream and rip your mike off."

SATELLITES and SHUTTLES

The world's first communication satellite was not, as is commonly supposed, *Telstar*, but *SCORE* (Signal Communications Orbital Relay Equipment), which was developed by the U.S. Army. *SCORE* was launched onboard an Atlas rocket on December 18, 1958, by NASA, but the satellite's batteries failed after only twelve days.

NASA launched *Telstar* in 1962 to relay telephone and data transmissions between the USA, the UK, and France.

And another thing . . .

The first musical single by a British band to reach number one on the U.S. charts was the 1962 instrumental "Telstar" by the Tornados (in the USA—Tornadoes), which was named after the satellite.

The first commercial communications satellite was *Intelsat 1*, which was also known as *Early Bird*. *Early Bird* was launched in April 1965 by an international consortium led by the USA. It was the first satellite to be placed in geosynchronous orbit, meaning it returned to precisely the same place at the same time every day. It remains in orbit today, but has been deactivated.

In 1962, NASA planned and designed the first manned, reuseable space vehicle, named *X20 Dyna Soar*, which was to be launched from a Titan 3 rocket. Neil Armstrong was one of the pilots, but the project was abandoned.

The first effective reusable space vehicle, commonly known as a space shuttle, was *Columbia*, which was first launched April 12, 1981. On its twenty-eighth mission in 2003, *Columbia* disintegrated on reentry to the Earth's atmosphere, and was lost. There were no survivors.

FIRST PRIVATE SPACECRAFT

On June 23, 2004, *Space Ship One*, designed by American aviation pioneer Burt Rutan (b. 1943) with pilot Mike Melvill (b. 1941) at the controls, crossed the frontier of space at 62.21 miles above sea level. Melvill was a mere 410 feet above the boundary of the Earth's atmosphere, but it was enough to enter the record books as the first privately funded and manned spacecraft.

Previous privately funded space travel ventures by Orbital Sciences and the Civilian Space Exploration Team had successfully produced spacecraft, but these had been unmanned.

MARS

The first man or woman to go to Mars is said to be walking somewhere on the Earth right now.

According to NASA, new space vehicles combining the best of the Apollo and shuttle technologies will be going to the Moon carrying four astronauts at a time. The Moon will be used as a staging post to launch a mission to Mars carrying six crew members. NASA's mission timetable includes the return of astronauts to the Moon in 2018 after a gap of forty-six years.

Sport and Leisure

BORN IN THE USA

BASKETBALL

Basketball is unique in that, unlike all other major sports, it did not evolve out of a group activity with long historical roots. Instead, basketball was invented by a single person, fairly recently.

In the winter of 1891, Dr. James Naismith (1861–1939), athletic director at the YMCA Training School in Springfield, Massachusetts, was faced with the problem of finding a sport to play indoors during the cold winter months. He wanted the sport to require skill, mobility, and ingenuity, rather than mere brute strength.

Naismith set out to create a game that could be played on a small sports area, and within fourteen days, had managed to devise a set of rules governing what would become basketball.

The first basketball games took place in late 1891 and were played with a soccer ball. The baskets for the first game, which were provided by the school janitor, were peach baskets with closed ends. This meant that play had to stop for the ball to be recovered from the basket by hand after every goal.

Basketball's popularity spread rapidly through the YMCA movement in many nations, and the sport was introduced into the Olympic program in 1936.

COUNTRY CLUB

Country clubs are an American invention and are rare in other parts of the world. They generally combine a few sports—usually golf, tennis, and swimming—with other social activities such as fine dining and cardplaying. Country clubs are places for (rich) friends and families to spend leisure time together.

"The Country Club," located in Brookline, Massachusetts, was founded in 1882 and is the oldest country club in the United States. Never referred to as "Brookline" Country Club, always "The Country Club," it holds an important place in golf history for a number of reasons. First, The Country Club was one of the five charter clubs in the foundation of the United States Golf Association, and has played host to several USGA tournaments. Second, one of the championships hosted by the club was the famous 1913 United States Open. This championship, which was won by then-unknown local amateur Francis Ouimet (1893–1967), played a major part in the growth of golf's popularity in the United States.

Coming into the championship, the two favorites were both English legends: Harry Vardon (1870–1937), who had won the 1900 U.S. Open and the British Open four times, and Ted Ray (1877–1943), the then-reigning British Open champion. Amazingly, after seventy-two holes, the English golfers found themselves tied with a twenty-year-old amateur who had grown up right across the street from the course, and had been a caddie at the club. In the eighteen-hole play-off the next day, Ouimet defeated the two professionals in front of a large gallery, and the resulting newspaper stories captured the imagination of the American public. The number of golfers in the country almost quadrupled in the subsequent ten years, as did the number of golf courses.

FRISBEE

The Frisbee has established a unique position in American culture; its popularity did not spread in the "world-dominating" way that yo-yos and hula hoops did, but it has remained consistently popular long after the appeal of similar toys wore off.

The Frisbie Pie Company (1871–1958) of Bridgeport, Connecticut, made pies that were sold to many New England colleges. At some point, playful college students discovered that the empty pie tins could be tossed and caught, providing endless hours of sport.

Many colleges have claimed to be the home of "he who was first to fling." Yale College has argued that in 1820, an undergraduate named Elihu Frisbie grabbed a passing collection tray from the chapel and flung it out into the campus, thereby becoming the true inventor of the Frisbee. That tale is dubious, as the "Frisbie's Pies" origin is much better documented.

Walter Frederick Morrison claims that it was a popcorn can lid that he tossed with his girlfriend (and later wife) Lu at a 1937 Thanksgiving Day gathering in Los Angeles that inspired his interest in developing a commercially produced flying disc. In 1946 he sketched out plans for a disc he called the Whirlo-Way, which, codeveloped and financed by Warren Franscioni in 1948, became the very first commercially produced plastic flying disc, marketed under the name Pipco Flyin-Saucer. Morrison had just returned to the United States after World War II, where he had been a prisoner in the infamous Stalag 13. His partnership with Franscioni, who was also a war veteran, ended in 1950, before their product had achieved any real success.

In 1955, to cash in on the public's growing fascination with UFOs, Morrison produced a new plastic flying disc called the Pluto Platter, which became the design basis for later flying discs. In 1957, Wham-O bought the rights to Pluto Platters from Morrison and began production of more discs (still marketed as Pluto Platters). The next year, Morrison was awarded U.S. Design Patent #183,626 for his flying disc.

In 1957, Wham-O cofounder Richard Knerr, in search of a catchy new name to help increase sales, coincidentally gave the disks the brand name "Frisbee" (pronounced the same as "Frisbie"), after a contemporary comic strip called *Mr. Frisbie.* The man who was behind the Frisbee's international success, however, was "Steady" Eddie Headrick, Wham-O's new general manager and vice president of marketing. Headrick also redesigned the Pluto Platter by reworking the rim height, disc shape, diameter, weight, and plastics, creating a controllable disc that could be thrown more accurately. He patented the changes, which became known as the "Rings of Headrick."

Sales soared for the toy, which was marketed as a new sport. In 1964 the first "professional" model went on sale. Headrick patented the new design as the Frisbee patent (highlighting the "Rings of Headrick") and marketed and pushed the professional model Frisbee and the related sport. Before selling the company to Mattel, Wham-O had produced and sold over 100 million Frisbees.

MONOPOLY

Monopoly is the bestselling board game of all time, and has millions of regular players worldwide.

In 1904, Lizzie Phillips (1866–1948) created and patented a board game called The Landlord's Game. The idea of this game was to illustrate some taxation theories and to highlight the negative aspects of private monopolies. It sounds more like an economics exercise than a board game, but The Landlord's Game was the precursor to Monopoly.

Twenty-five years later, Charles Darrow (1879–1967) lost his job as a result of the Great Depression. He began to work on the board game that was to become Monopoly, and in 1934, after its rejection by Parker Brothers for "52 design errors," he began to produce the game himself. Apart from name changes to certain squares, it is largely the game we play today. In 1935 Darrow was granted a patent on Monopoly, and Parker Bros. agreed to take a license from him to mass-produce and distribute it. Within twelve months, they were selling more than 20,000 Monopoly sets every week.

There appears to be an endless appetite for this unique board game. It is now available in 103 countries and thirty-seven languages, with total volume sales of games now above 200 million. It is estimated that 500 million people worldwide have played Monopoly since its introduction, and over 5 billion little green houses have been "built" since 1935.

And another thing . . .

During World War II a special edition of Monopoly was produced and shipped to prisoners of war in Germany. Some of the games contained real money, maps, and other items that would be useful if prisoners managed to escape. The International Red Cross distributed the games.

SCRABBLE

In 1931 Alfred Mosher Butts (1899–1993) of Pennsylvania was an unemployed architect living in Depression-era America. Having little else to occupy his time, he set out to design a board game.

Butts was a big fan of crossword puzzles, which were hugely popular at the time, but he wanted his new game to incorporate an element of chance, as well as require a skill for words. The game he came up with was called Lexico. Though it was very similar to the sometime winner Scrabble, Butts's patent application for Lexico was turned down, and no manufacturer could be found to develop and market the game.

Butts changed the name several times, at one point calling it Criss-Crosswords. His patent application was turned down for a second time, and yet again no manufacturer would take it up.

Butts needed capital, so he sold his rights to the game to an enthusiast, James Brunot, accepting a royalty for each game sold. Brunot made a few minor changes to the design, but the biggest change of all was the inspired renaming of the game to Scrabble.

In 1948 Brunot trademarked Scrabble, and 1952 brought a big commercial breakthrough when the chairman of Macy's, the world's biggest department store, found that Scrabble was not stocked in his store. He is famous for the question he put to a meeting of his executives, "What do you mean Macy's don't stock Scrabble?" Macy's quickly placed a major order and supported a nationwide promotional campaign. Sales took off. In 1953, Brunot shipped six thousand sets per week, and with his burgeoning order book, he licensed the manufacturing and distribution to Selchow and Righter of New York.

More than 100 million Scrabble sets have been sold worldwide. It is sold in 121 countries and twenty-nine languages, and in 1991 London hosted the first World Championship of Scrabble. By the age of ninety-one, Alfred Butts had lived to see the game he had struggled so hard to launch half a century earlier finally being played around the world. Even Queen Elizabeth II plays.

SKATEBOARD

Today's skateboard is an ingenious combination of strength and flexibility. With its innovative engineering principles and eye-catching board designs, skateboarding's popularity has spread throughout the world since the first great boom in America in the 1970s. In the intervening years, as the sport has grown, a whole industry has swollen to match the demand, with manufacturing plants, retail outlets, and national and world championships. Special skate parks have been built in even the smallest villages.

The skateboard developed out of the desire of Californian surfers to be able to duplicate the feeling of surfing, but on land. The first boards were simple assemblies of roller-skate wheels attached to a plank of wood, and in 1958 the first retail skateboard was brought to market by Bill and Mark Richards of Dana Point, California.

The current generation of skateboards is dominated by street skating, and in 2004 the International Association of Skateboard Companies created a "Go Skateboarding Day" to further promote the activity. It is now so popular that a whole new language, unintelligible to outsiders, has sprung up within the skateboarding community.

SKEET SHOOTING

Skeet is a competitive sport in which participants use a shotgun to try to shoot down clay disks that are flung into the air from traps set at various angles.

The origin of skeet shooting goes back to Clock Shooting, invented by Charles Davies in 1915. The Clock Shooting course was a twenty-five-yard-radius circle with the trap at 12 o'clock. Targets were thrown over 6 o'clock, and the idea of the game was to improve the skills of the shooter from a variety of different angles.

In 1923, the American author William Harnden Foster (1886–1941) modified the course by cutting it in half and placing a second trap at 6 o'clock. Foster was eager to create a national sport and introduced it in 1926 in the main sporting magazines of the day. In the article, he offered a prize of $100 to anyone who could come up with a suitable new name for the sport.

The winner was Gertrude Halbert, who chose "skeet," the Scandinavian word for "shoot."

In 1968 skeet shooting became an Olympic sport.

SPEED-DATING

Los Angeles–based Rabbi Yaacov Deyo of the pro-Israel organization Aish HaTorah is credited with inventing speed-dating, which is a formalized round-robin matchmaking process. He saw it as a way of helping Jewish singles to meet suitable partners, and registered the single word SpeedDating as a trademark.

Speed-dating events allow a specified time, usually between three and eight minutes, for each potential couple to meet and decide whether or not they are interested in each other. The events, which are very fast-paced, match each participant with several potential partners, and they are allowed to discuss anything except careers or where they live.

In 1998, the first speed-dating session took place at Pete's Café in Beverly Hills, California. Following television advertisements that publicized it as a glamorous, modern activity, it quickly spread beyond the Jewish community, and was nationwide by 2000.

BOBBY JONES (1902–1971)

A country that can produce Robert Tyre Jones must have something very special in its soul.

Jones bestrode the world of golf in the 1920s like a colossus, but his triumphs were achieved with immutable modesty—no fist pumping, no jumping in the air and no screaming and shouting. He never complained when he lost and never bragged when he won.

An example of his belief in the sanctity of sporting ideals occurred as he called a penalty on himself when his ball moved as he was addressing it. At the time, he was in contention for the U.S. Open Championship, and eventually lost the title in a play-off. As his ball had been in deep rough at the time, no one else could have seen it move except Jones, and when he was congratulated on his sporting behavior after the event, he would have none of it. He said, "You might as well congratulate a man for not robbing a bank."

"But no one would ever have known," came the response from a reporter.

"I would," said Jones.

His was the purest form of sporting behavior yet known and he was given the rare privilege of two ticker tape parades in New York, in 1926 and 1930.

As a competitor, Jones still has no equal, and unlike other sporting records that are routinely broken, it is unlikely his feats will ever be approached, let alone surpassed. Despite only ever competing as an amateur, he established himself as the finest golfer of his generation and certainly the finest amateur golfer of all time.

To recap his career, Bobby Jones won the U.S. Open four times, the U.S. Amateur five times, the British Open three times, and the British Amateur once. In his impregnable year of 1930, he achieved the Grand Slam, winning the Open and Amateur Championships of the United States and Great Britain, in the same year, a feat so stunning that the odds against it being repeated are probably incalculable. Bobby Jones retired from competitive golf in 1930 at the age of twenty-eight, with no new worlds to conquer.

His name will be forever woven into the fabric of golf and the American psyche. Three quarters of a century after he made history, no other golfer has even come close. Only six have completed a "Half Slam," and no one has yet done three out of the four. However, as a man, Jones achieved much more than his great sporting feats.

He earned a BSc in mechanical engineering and a BA in English literature, and was also a member of the bar. In fact, he was a practicing lawyer during the years he was playing golf.

At the age of forty-six he was diagnosed with syringomyelia, a disease of the spine that causes intense pain and eventually paralysis. Jones announced the news to his friends soon after the diagnosis, and, not wishing to be a burden in any way, said, "We will never speak of this again."

It almost seemed that the gods, who had bestowed such gifts on their chosen one, had decided to exact a full measure of payment. And then some.

Only two Americans have been made Freemen of the City of St. Andrews, the ancient ecclesiastical capital of Scotland. The great polymath Benjamin Franklin was the first in 1759, and Robert Tyre Jones was the second in 1958.

> "You can make a lot of money in this game. Ask my ex wives. Both of them are so rich neither of their husbands work."
>
> **—Lee Trevino** (U.S. golf champion)

AMERICANS WHO CHANGED THEIR SPORTS
Dick Fosbury (High Jump)

Before Dick Fosbury (b. 1947) revolutionized the high jump with his "back down" style, jumpers crossed the bar either facedown toward the ground, as in the "straddle" jump, or on their side using the Western Roll. Fosbury took the new style and made it his own, although Bruce Quande of the USA is known to have used the technique as early as 1963. Fosbury achieved immortality after the technique was named the "Fosbury Flop" in his honor.

In 1968, Fosbury won the NCAA Championship and the U.S. Olympic trials using his new technique. Later that year at the Olympic Games in Mexico City, in front of a worldwide audience numbering almost half a billion people, Fosbury broke the Olympic record and won the gold medal for the high jump with a height of 2.24 meters.

In Mexico, Fosbury was the only competitor using the Fosbury Flop, and many commentators queried whether the technique was legal. By 1980, thirteen of the sixteen finalists were using it. Today it is difficult to find a high jumper who doesn't use the Fosbury Flop.

John McEnroe (Tennis)

John McEnroe (b. 1959) didn't so much change the way tennis was played, but more the way competitors behaved while they were playing. His seemingly out-of-control rants were the type of behavior that had never before been witnessed in professional sportsmen. The nearest to this behavior was in demonstration sports like professional wrestling, in which the contestants were expected to scream and rant, not only at their opponent but also at the referee. McEnroe took tennis to the same level.

Before McEnroe emerged as the "enfant terrible" of the tennis world, the great champions such as Rod Laver, Bill Tilden, Arthur Ashe, and Bjorn Borg accepted the occasional wrong line call, and miscalled foot faults as "rub of the green." They accepted with good grace that, over the course of time, the good and the bad tend to even themselves out.

McEnroe was having none of it.

Jimmy Connors before him had started the routine questioning of umpires' decisions, but McEnroe took it to the point of massive aggression and screaming accusations. On one famous occasion he smashed his racket across the table holding the water glasses, sending broken glass and water flying across the court. The authorities failed to penalize him for behavior that would have seen him dismissed from the field of play in most other sports. Working on the basis that the crowd had come to watch him play, and that the controlling bodies would never back the on-court officials, McEnroe figured he could get away with it. And he did.

Nowadays the ruling bodies of tennis have had to set up rules to accommodate line-call questioning. Every competitor in professional tennis routinely uses up his or her allowance of queries, and most of this can be attributed to the activity of the so-called superbrat.

Parry O'Brien (Shot Put)

Parry O'Brien (1932–2007), is not well-remembered today, but there was a time in the 1950s when he changed the technique of shot putting to such a degree that after he had proved its value, all other competitors copied him.

Until O'Brien's fresh look at his sport, the technique had been to tuck the sixteen-pound metal shot under or at the side of the chin and begin the throw facing at right angles to the intended direction. This method called on strong arm power, but did not fully utilize the other main muscle groups.

O'Brien's technique was to begin the throw by facing the opposite direction from the target. The first action of the actual throw was to take as deep a knee-bend as practical and shoot at maximum speed across the throwing circle toward the target. On landing around the center of the circle, the thrower was still in the full knee-bend position, but moving toward the target. At this point the thrower was able to unleash the pent-up power of the lower limbs and upper torso, in a chain reaction, with each component building the speed of the shot above its predecessor, until the arm delivered the final powerful "shove."

From 1953 until 1959, he broke the world record seventeen times, becoming the first man through the 59-, 60-, 61-, 62-, and 63-foot barriers. He won two Olympic golds (1952 and 1956) and one silver (1960).

Jesse Owens (Track and Field)

In the infamous Berlin Olympics of 1936, Jesse Owens won the 100- and 200-meter sprints and the long jump. He won a fourth gold medal in the 4 x 100 meter relay. These feats alone elevated Owens to iconic status, and it was claimed that he was the greatest athlete of all time. However, it is because the behavior of another man that Owens is best remembered today.

Adolf Hitler shamed his nation when he refused to acknowledge the supreme achievements of Jesse Owens. Owens was an African American, and Hitler, with his deep hatred of nonwhite people, could not bring himself to meet or shake hands with him. In the long jump, Owens had fought a classic battle against the blond, blue-eyed German champion Lutz Long, and won the gold medal by a few fractions of an inch. Hitler could not even bear to watch, flouncing out of the stadium with his phalanx of stooges.

With his quiet dignity and his refusal to be drawn into the controversy, Jesse Owens did an enormous amount to overcome the damage caused by the actions of the dictator. His behavior elevated track and field to the forefront of the political debate, and helped to overcome racial prejudice in sport. Future athletes such as Tommie Smith and John Carlos were to take more dramatic steps in the cause of race relations, but Jesse Owens had paved the way.

Arnold Palmer (Golf)

Arnold Palmer (b. 1929), more than any other competitor, brought the middle-class sport of golf to the masses. His fame coincided with the Television Age, and his feats were broadcast to greater numbers than any previous golfer. At his peak Palmer was one of the so-called Big Three who ruled the world of golf. The other two were Gary Player and Jack Nicklaus.

People respected Nicklaus for his immense talent. They would stand back in amazement as he hit shot after shot that even the greatest golfers could not match. His towering iron shots seemed to climb forever and his drives looked as if they had been fired from a cannon.

The golfing public admired Player, who stood only 5'7" tall. By the sheer strength of his will, he managed to triumph against men who dwarfed him. He won matches when all seemed lost. Those same people who respected Nicklaus and admired Player felt a different emotion for Palmer. They worshipped him.

Arnie, as he was known, seemed to embody everything important in an American sportsman: high skills, striking looks, the ability to win under pressure, and the occasional lapse of vulnerability. He possessed a golf swing that looked like a man chopping down trees; he was everyman. Compared with the elegant swings of the past champions he looked like a mere hacker with attitude. But when charisma genes were being distributed among the athletes of the world, Arnold Palmer got almost everybody else's share.

He electrified the watching millions across the globe, and when he hitched up his pants—his "trademark" gesture—pulses raced. He was the first star who seemed able to conjure shots for the dramatic moment. The immense carry across a lake, the bunker shot holed, the winning birdie on the last hole of the U.S. Masters. He did them all, and he did them looking like the man from the local golf course, not the best golfer in the world.

"Arnie's Army," his dedicated followers, materialized in massive numbers wherever in the world their hero was weaving his magic, and golf changed forever with the advent of Arnold Palmer.

Karsten Solheim (Golf)

Karsten Solheim (1911–2000) was no champion golfer, but he revolutionized golf as surely as if he had won the Grand Slam.

Solheim didn't pick up a golf club until he was forty-two, when he was invited one day by some work colleagues to join them for a game. Although he was able to strike the ball reasonably, he found putting very difficult. He decided to apply engineering principles to the design of a better putter.

After a series of failed experiments, he came up with the "ANSER," the first in a line of Ping putters. He decided to start making a few for sale. At first he had difficulty convincing professionals to try the new type of putter, as it was rather strange looking with the weight of the blade placed at each end of the blade rather than being evenly distributed as in the traditional blade. Eventually Julius Boros (1920–1994), at the age of forty-seven, used a Ping putter to win the 1967 Phoenix Open, a main event on the US PGA Tour. With the publicity this attracted, and the explosive demand for his new putter, Solheim felt confident enough to resign from his job at General Electric and set up his own golf club manufacturing company.

In 1969 he introduced a range of irons that incorporated the same engineering principle, by positioning the weight at each end of the blade. The effect of this simple idea was to increase the effective hitting area of the blade. The "sweet spot" felt bigger and allowed golfers to "get away with" less-than-perfect shots, but with similar results.

This revolutionary design reversed hundreds of years of traditional golf club design.

Later, the principle of perimeter weighting was applied to woods, to give golfers a far greater margin for error. Shots that previously would have landed in trouble were now landing within a small margin of a perfect shot. The effect was that golfers could now afford to hit the ball harder than previously, and the ball consequently traveled much farther.

This had the unforeseen effect years later of making some golf courses too easy, and the occasional hole redundant.

All golf club manufacturers now follow Karsten Solheim's original thinking.

Babe Zaharias (All-Around Athlete)

Babe Zaharias (1911–1956) was probably the greatest sportswoman of all time.

She is named in the *Guinness Book of Records* as the most versatile athlete ever, along with Lottie Dod. In both 1949 and 1999, the Associated Press voted her as the Woman Athlete of the Twentieth Century. In 2000, *Sports Illustrated* named her as the second on their list of the greatest female athletes of all time, behind Jackie Joyner-Kersee. She is the top-ranked woman, at number ten, on EPSN's list of the top fifty athletes of the twentieth century, and in 2000 was named by *Golf Digest* magazine as the seventeenth best golfer of either sex. The only woman ranked ahead of her was Mickey Wright at number nine.

Her sporting career embraced basketball, at which she was named on the All-American squad, and track and field, in which she won two Olympic gold medals and a silver medal in the 1932 games. She came late to golf, but went on to win every championship available to her.

In 1938, Zaharias became the first woman to contest a men's tournament on the US PGA circuit. She failed to make the "cut" in that event and it would be almost another sixty years until another woman, Annika Sorenstam, would try. In 1945, she played in the Los Angeles Open on the men's PGA Tour and made the cut, the only woman in history to do so.

Only forty-five and at the peak of her powers, "Babe" Zaharias lost her life to colon cancer. She had opened up the world of women's sport, especially golf, and was renowned for her exceptional sportsmanship. She still serves as a cultural icon today.

> "She is beyond all belief until you see her perform . . . then you finally understand that you are looking at the most flawless section of muscle harmony, of complete mental and physical coordination, the world of sport has ever seen."
>
> **—Grantland Rice, sportswriter**

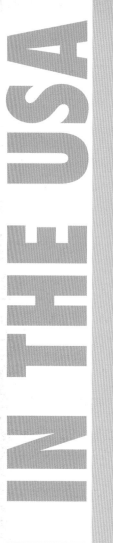

Money

"You can't force anyone to love you or to lend you money."

—Jewish proverb

Society without a form of money depends on barter and the chance occurrence of having precisely the equal value of barter goods to exchange in any transaction, the so-called double coincidence.

Money itself is "only" a man-made concept. It provides a convenient means of exchange and a way of storing value. Confidence in a person's ability to exchange the "dollar in your pocket" for a desired item is the basis of the value of money. Pretty much all tangible goods such as houses, cars, and food have a monetary value. Even intangibles such as mental health, prison reform, art, and the space race have monetary values attached.

Over the last 100 years, the United States has been the world's greatest creator of new wealth (money), the U.S. dollar has become the world's reserve currency, and its financial muscle was used to draw back the Iron Curtain.

Most of the exotic new ways of raising finance originated in the USA and the convenience of being able to pay for anything almost anywhere, with just a small piece of plastic, was likewise invented in the USA.

"There are three faithful friends: an old wife, an old dog, and ready money."

—Benjamin Franklin

U.S. Dollar

The U.S. dollar originated immediately after the USA achieved its independence from Britain. Until that time, the currency was the British pound. There was a shortage of coinage at that time, and Spanish pesos, also called dollars, were in circulation. It was decided in 1792 to adopt the dollar as the unit of currency rather than retain the English pound. The first U.S. Mint was established in Philadelphia and began producing coins in 1794.

Throughout most of the twentieth century, the U.S. dollar was the world's reserve currency, against which all other currencies were gauged.

And another thing . . .

The term "dollar" comes from the Czech currency "thaler," which was first minted in 1519. Thaler (phonetically "tarler") was mispronounced in England as "dollar."

The $ symbol has an uncertain origin. One theory claims it derives from taking the two initials of the U.S., superimposing the U on top of the S and removing the horizontal lower portion of the U. There are at least six convincing theories, but no definitive origin.

The first bank in the USA was the Bank of North America, which opened its doors in 1782, having been proposed, chartered, and incorporated in 1781. The first central bank in the USA was the Bank of the United States, which was formed in 1791. Its Congressional Charter expired in 1811.

Alexander Hamilton (1757–1804) is regarded as the "father" of banking in the USA and the patron saint of American economic philosophy. He was the first secretary of the treasury and founded the Bank of America. Hamilton also founded the U.S. Coast Guard, which collected excise duties. He was killed in a duel with Aaron Burr (1756–1836), the U.S. vice president at the time, over some insulting words Hamilton allegedly said about Burr. After the governorship of New York had gone to his own candidate, Morgan Lewis, Hamilton was reported in the *Albany Letter* as expressing "a still more despicable opinion" of Burr, the defeated candidate. Hamilton told Burr that he could not recall saying such a thing, and refused to withdraw or retract the words. He met his death with Burr's first shot.

Alexander Hamilton

NEW YORK STOCK EXCHANGE (NYSE)

The world's largest stock exchange opened for business on May 17, 1792, with twenty-four brokers. The founding document of the New York Stock Exchange is known as the Buttonwood Agreement, since the brokers signed the document under a buttonwood tree in Wall Street, Manhattan.

There are now 2,800 companies listed on the NYSE, with a total market value of almost 20 trillion dollars, greater than the total amount of money circulating in the USA. (A trillion is 1,000 billion, or, to put it another way, a million million—$1,000,000,000,000).

WALL STREET

Wall Street, an otherwise unremarkable street in Manhattan, is the financial epicenter of not just the nation-state of America, but also the rest of the world. No other single street in history has reserved to itself such awesome financial muscle.

In 1653, a fortified wall was built along the northern boundary of the New Amsterdam settlement, as the defense against some Native American tribes. By 1685, Wall Street had been laid out along the line of the old fortified wall.

The statue of the charging bull was originally sited in front of the New York Stock Exchange building, and came to symbolize a powerful bull market.

BRETTON WOODS

At the end of World War II, it was not only the vanquished European countries (Germany, Austria, and Italy) that were bankrupt but also the forty-four Allied nations, in particular Britain, Holland, France, and Belgium.

The United States, which was among the few solvent countries left in the world, set new standards of decency, broad thinking, and statesmanship at the United Nations Monetary and Financial Conference held in 1944 at Bretton Woods, New Hampshire. More than 700 delegates from the forty-four Allied countries attended, and agreements were signed that led to the formation of the General Agreement on Tariffs and Trade (GATT), the International Bank for Reconstruction and Development (IBRD), and the International Monetary Fund (IMF).

The victors in a war normally take the opportunity to exact a measure of vengeance, either by financial or physical enslavement. Considering the atrocities performed by the defeated Nazi regime and the high financial cost of the war, it might have been understandable if America had insisted on large-scale reparations along the lines of those following World War I.

For the first time in history, a nation-state decided to do the precise opposite.

America was the only country left that could provide funding on a scale large enough to be meaningful. It was only America that could make a difference. In 1945, the USA lent Britain $3.8 billion and France $1.0 billion. Between 1948 and 1954, it gave further advances totaling over $16 billion to European countries, including former enemies, to promote economic stability. Sums such as these were enormous for the time.

The United States, in effect, averted the paralysis of the world's capitalism.

ELECTRONIC MONEY

The first time money became transferable from one bank account to another by electronic means was in 1871. Western Union pioneered the telegraphic transfer of money in the USA, and in the intervening years has maintained a prominent position in this area of finance.

PLASTIC MONEY (CREDIT CARD)

The use of credit cards originated in the USA in the 1920s. As a way of retaining customer loyalty, oil companies and hotel chains began to issue credit cards for use by existing customers. The cards were only for use at the companies' own outlets.

In 1950, Diners Club issued the first universal credit card. Diners Club cards could be used by the public at any outlet that would accept credit cards in settlement of bills.

The American Express card followed in 1958.

INTERNET BANKING

Internet banking is the logical evolution of the electronic (telegraphic) money transfers pioneered by Western Union in the nineteenth century. With Internet banking, customers are able to gain direct access to their bank accounts at any time to check balances and transactions and to make direct payments to other accounts. Paper transactions are almost eliminated.

In 1990, Wells Fargo Bank of America became the first bank in the world to complete an Internet banking transaction.

ATM (AUTOMATIC TELLER MACHINE)

The ATM device, which is seen on streets throughout the world, was first developed by the prolific U.S. inventor Luther Simjian (1905–1997).

In 1939, the world's first ATM, the Bankmatic, opened for business at the City Bank of New York. After a six-month trial period, City Bank (now Citicorp) reported that there was little demand for the new machine and withdrew it from service.

Simjian believed that the only people using his machine were prostitutes, gamblers, and others who did not wish to deal face-to-face with bank tellers.

ROBBER BARON

The term "robber baron" actually comes from medieval times, when unscrupulous lords charged exorbitant tolls on the River Rhine in Germany. The practice was illegal but tolerated.

In nineteenth-century America the term "robber baron" was resurrected to mean any industrialist or banker who dominated his industry. With a young, vigorous economy in which new industries seemed to sprout every week, America was the one place in the world where a determined businessman could climb to a position of total dominance of an industry. Business was covered in the press and in books as never before, and people felt that many of the new tycoons, who had acquired great fortunes, had done so by unfair business practices. The historian Allan Nevins (1890–1971) maintained that the economy of the United States had risen to prominence as a direct result of the work of the robber barons. Nevins believed they brought order and stability to an unstable business environment.

> "I believe that the able industrial leader, who creates wealth and employment, is more worthy of historical notice than politicians or soldiers."
>
> **—J. Paul Getty** (1892–1976)

Businesses and Brands

> "The chief business of the American people is business."
>
> **—U.S. President Calvin Coolidge**
>
> (1872–1933)

> "The 20th century has surely been without parallel in all of human history. Nowhere have all the changes been so remarkable as in the American economy."
>
> **—Paul Volcker**
>
> (b. 1927), Federal Reserve Chairman 1979–1987

Several American brands have become household names all over the world. The most prominent of these can be seen on high streets, in cafés, on sports fields, in our homes, and going into your gas tank. American brands are seen on public roads in cities across the globe. They end up on your toothbrush or provide access to the information superhighway. They are so ubiquitous you hardly notice them.

In consumer markets, American businesses have always possessed exceptional marketing punch. Their skilled approach, honed almost to a fine art in the U.S. domestic market, has enabled them to capture major market segments in other countries. One example is the soft-drinks industry of India, in which more than 90 percent of the whole market is shared between the two American cola giants, Coke and Pepsi. Their portrayal of "American glamour" is unmatchable by the local soft-drinks companies, who can hardly get a look in.

Another example is the software known as Microsoft Word. To launch it, Microsoft brought in the marketing big guns, who bundled Word in with a suite of other products. Against the tide of competing products, it has been established as the dominant word-processing software across the whole of the high-tech industry.

It is not only in consumer products that the great American brands are dominant. Chemical products such as Kevlar and nylon dominate their areas of application and are supplied to consumer and industrial product manufacturers. These are world-dominating materials that end up as components within other finished products, but are recognized as brands themselves. Similarly, Intel processors are incorporated into most of the world's computers, becoming by their presence a major part of the branding exercise.

The immense American market offers a unique opportunity for American entrepreneurs to bring in innovative products and services. American consumers welcome the new and the novel, whereas the dominant culture of Europe encourages consumers to resist change.

With the comfort of their solid home base, companies such as Microsoft, Coca-Cola, McDonald's, and Heinz do not have to shelter behind the parapet, but march out into overseas territories.

Here are the best of the best.

COCA-COLA

Coca-Cola, the giant among world brands, is now sold in 200 countries—a far cry from its modest origins.

In 1886, using an old family recipe, Dr. John Pemberton (1831–1888) a pharmacist of Atlanta, Georgia, concocted the formula for a nonalcoholic drink. In one of those strange turns of fate, Pemberton was actually trying to develop a beverage to stop headaches and promote calm, but instead produced what would become the biggest-selling soft drink in history.

His bookkeeper, Frank Robinson (1845–1923), came up with the name Coca-Cola. Robinson had highly developed penmanship—he even scripted the flowing letters we see in the Coca-Cola logo today. It has become the most recognized trademark in the world.

In May 1886, the first ever Coca-Cola was dispensed from the soda fountain in Jacob's Pharmacy in Atlanta. Annual sales that year amounted to the not-very-promising total of just fifty dollars (which would be around $1000 today).

In 1889, another Atlanta pharmacist named Asa Candler (1851–1929) bought the formula and rights from Pemberton for $2,300. Candler was aware of the Coca-Cola drink, and wanted to develop a product with a known name that could be sold in large quantities

Aggressive marketing by Candler kick-started the sales of Coca-Cola, and by the late 1890s, it had become one of the most popular drinks in America. Sales rocketed by 4,000 percent between 1890 and 1900, and the brand went on over the next forty years to become a cultural icon.

One of history's most enduring advertising campaigns was designed to remind the public that Coca-Cola was not just a summer drink, but for all year round. In 1931, the artist Haddon Sundblom developed this idea. Working closely from the image of Santa Claus that had first been painted in 1862 by the Civil War cartoonist Thomas Nast, Sundblom painted Santa as a jolly, plump fellow in a red coat, drinking from a bottle of Coca-Cola, surrounded by a toy train set. The train set was clearly a Christmas present for a young boy. The Coca-Cola Christmas campaign, featuring Santa Claus in that form, ran until 1964, an unprecedented thirty-three years.

As the sales of bottled soft drinks in America began to overtake the soda fountain, Candler realized he would need to engage the services of local soft-drink bottlers to give the sales of Coca-Cola more regional loyalty. As innovative as ever, he entered into licensing agreements across America with local bottling companies to sell them Coca-Cola syrup. They then converted the syrup into a fizzy drink and distributed it within their agreed territories. The first bottled Coca-Cola was sold in 1894, but the soda fountain continued to play a role in the soft-drinks industry until around 1960. Sales of the bottled drink finally overtook those dispensed in fountains.

Coke's grip on the world's soft-drinks market began to tighten when bottling plants were opened all over Europe during World War II.

BusinessWeek and Interbrand compile an annual ranking of the world's most valuable brands. In 2008, for the seventh year in a row, Coca-Cola was rated as the world's most valuable brand.

And another thing . . .

The so-called Coca-Cola Formula is the secret recipe for Coca-Cola, and is known to only a handful of senior executives of the company. Despite outsiders using modern scientific analysis procedures to "reverse engineer" the formula, the Coca-Cola Company insists that the correct recipe has never been found.

PEPSI-COLA

In the early 1890s, a North Carolina pharmacist named Caleb Bradham (1867–1934) devised the formula for a soft drink that he began to market under the brand name Brad's Drink. Bradham acquired the name Pep Kola in 1898 and immediately changed it to Pepsi-Cola, which he trademarked in 1903. In 1931, with the whole economy in the middle of the Great Depression, and after suffering losses on wildly fluctuating sugar prices, the company went bankrupt. Roy C. Megargel bought the Pepsi trademark, but eight years later, the company went bankrupt again.

Pepsi was then bought by Charles Guth, the president of Loft Inc. Loft was a candy manufacturer with retail stores that featured soda fountains. One of Guth's motivations for buying Pepsi was to replace Coca-Cola at his stores' fountains, after Coke had refused to give him a discount on syrup.

Guth arranged for Loft's chemists to reformulate the Pepsi-Cola syrup formula and the company began to steadily claw market share from its bigger rival, Coca-Cola. In the process, it also achieved cultural icon status, and in some territories, Pepsi outsells Coke.

Like Coca-Cola, Pepsi has always employed aggressive marketing techniques, and from 1984 its advertisements began to feature huge global stars such as Michael Jackson, Tina Turner, Van Halen, Ray Charles, and Mary J. Blige. With this seemingly simple strategy, Pepsi-Cola cemented itself into the consciousness of consumers around the world.

McDONALD'S

McDonald's is the world's largest chain of fast-food restaurants. Its global reach is so wide that it serves around 47 million people every day in 120 countries.

The business began in 1940, founded in San Bernardino, California by two brothers, Dick (1909–1998) and Mac (1902–1971) McDonald.

The McDonald brothers began to franchise their business, and in 1955, they took on their ninth franchisee, Ray Kroc (1902–1984). Kroc was so confident in the future for the McDonald business that he bought the equity from the McDonald brothers and began a massive expansion program.

Kroc oversaw immense growth in his business using the innovative franchise system that had been developed by the McDonalds. Today the company is the world's biggest chain of fast-food restaurants.

The fifty-billionth hamburger was sold in 1984. In a formal ceremony, it was cooked and served by Dick McDonald, the man who had cooked the very first one.

In the eyes of the world, the company has become the symbol of globalization and the spread of the American way of life. The brand's prominence has made McDonald's a topic of public debate about obesity and corporate ethics.

And another thing . . .

Ronald McDonald, who became the corporate mascot in 1963, is a real person and is still working in the hospitality industry in Tampa, Florida.

HEINZ

"Beanz Meanz Heinz"

—Heinz slogan

It was a natural: The three-word slogan that was the perfect model of simplicity and that was destined to travel the world, had been waiting there unused, for nearly 100 years.

In 1869, two young businessmen, Henry J. Heinz and L. Clarence Noble, decided to diversify out of their brick-making business. They decided to go into food production. They set up their business in Sharpsburg, Pennsylvania, and their first product was "Pure and Superior Horseradish." They bottled it in clear glass to show its purity and the foundation of their food empire was made, although at this stage the company name was Heinz & Noble. In 1876 they introduced tomato ketchup.

1892 was the year Heinz adopted the company slogan of "57 varieties." According to company history, Heinz had been on the train and as it was coming into a station when he spotted a shoe shop advertisement that boasted "21 Styles." With a little bit of artistic license, Heinz decided to use the same type of claim and settled on 57 Varieties, although his company already sold far more than that. Today, Heinz sells more than 1,300 varieties of food products worldwide.

The first step toward building a world brand came in 1896, when Heinz baked beans first hit the shelves in the UK, where they were sold as a luxury item in Fortnum & Mason in Piccadilly. Heinz now sells its products in 200 countries, and has become the world's fourth-biggest food and drink company. By 2007 sales had reached over $10 billion and the company was valued at $11 billion.

The TV jingle, "A million housewives every day, pick up a tin of beans and say, 'Beanz Meanz Heinz,'" was launched in 1961.

KFC

"Colonel" Harland David Sanders (1890–1980) was one of the more colorful American businessmen to emerge in the twentieth century. He had worked as a steamboat driver, railroad fireman, insurance salesman, and farmer. He enlisted in the U.S. Army, but only served as a private, not a colonel.

Sanders was a Kentucky Colonel, which is an honorary title bestowed by the state governor to people he considers to be worthy citizens. The title carries no duties and is not a paid position. Kentucky Colonel is not a military rank, but Sanders chose to refer to himself as "Colonel" as a way of self-promotion, even before starting KFC. He also liked to reflect his honorary title by dressing as a traditional "Southern gentleman," wearing a white suit and hat.

At the age of forty, Sanders was operating a gas station in Corbin, Kentucky, and began to offer cooked chicken dishes to his customers. The popularity of his food grew and he opened a restaurant, but some years later, when Interstate 75 was built nearby, his business suffered badly.

As a way out of his financial difficulties, he decided to offer franchises with his "secret recipe" for great-tasting fried chicken. At the age of sixty-five, Sanders was close to bankruptcy, but with the help of his first Social Security check, and with his secret recipe, Colonel Sanders set out on the road to sell his recipe and appoint franchisees.

Through the 1940s and 1950s chicken was a luxury food, but "Colonel" Sanders changed all that. He used the advertising slogan, "it's finger-lickin' good," and Kentucky Fried Chicken became the first of the great American franchised food companies to colonize overseas markets.

He opened his first franchise in 1952 at South Salt Lake, Utah, and by the turn of the century there were 16,000 KFC restaurants around the world.

And another thing . . .

There is only one complete copy of Colonel Sanders's secret recipe. An original from 1940, it contains precise amounts of eleven herbs and spices and is written in pencil on a single sheet of notepaper. The recipe remains heavily guarded and is known to only two people at any one time.

YAHOO!

Yahoo! was the first online navigational guide (search engine) to the World Wide Web.

The company began life as a student hobby and evolved to become a global brand. In the course of its growth, it changed the way people communicate with each other, the way they find and access information, and the way they make purchases. The founders, David Filo and Jerry Yang, were electrical engineering students at Stanford University. They started their guide in a campus trailer in February 1994 as a way to keep track of their own personal interests on the Internet. It was not long before the pair began spending more time on their favorite links than on their doctoral dissertations.

Eventually their lists became too long and unwieldy, and they set them into categories. When the categories themselves became too full, Filo and Yang developed subcategories and developed the "search engine" concept.

The original name of the Web site was Jerry and David's Guide to the World Wide Web. They began the search for a new name and settled on Yahoo! which is supposed to be an acronym for "Yet Another Hierarchical Officious Oracle." Nowadays Filo and Yang insist they selected the name because they liked the general definition of a yahoo: "rude, unsophisticated, uncouth." Interestingly, the first mention of "yahoo" in literature is in *Gulliver's Travels*, written by Jonathan Swift in 1726. Within weeks after they launched their guide, hundreds of people were accessing it, as the word spread among the close-knit

Internet community. By the end of 1994, Yahoo! had experienced its first million-hit day.

Due to the torrent of traffic and the enthusiastic reception Yahoo! was receiving, the founders knew they had a potential business on their hands. In March 1995, the pair incorporated the business and met with dozens of Silicon Valley venture capitalists. They eventually came across Sequoia Capital, the well-regarded firm whose most successful investments included Apple Computer, Atari, Oracle, and Cisco Systems. The company agreed to fund Yahoo! in April 1995 with an initial investment of nearly $2 million.

Realizing their new company had the potential to grow quickly, Jerry and David began to shop for a management team. They hired Tim Koogle as chief executive officer. Koogle was a veteran of Motorola and an alumnus of the Stanford engineering department. Jeffrey Mallett, founder of Novell's WordPerfect consumer division, was hired as chief operating officer. Between them they managed to secure a second round of funding in the fall of 1995 from investors, Reuters Ltd., and Softbank. Yahoo! launched a highly successful IPO in April 1996 with a total of forty-nine employees.

As of October 2007, the Yahoo! Web site was receiving an average of 3.4 billion page views per day and was the most visited Web site on the planet. In February 2008, Microsoft launched a bid to acquire Yahoo! for $44.6 billion. The board of Yahoo! turned the bid down. On November 30, 2008, with stock prices tumbling worldwide, Microsoft bid $20 billion for Yahoo!

GOOGLE

To traditional business owners and managers, the rise and rise of Google seems to defy gravity.

In 1996, Larry Page (b. 1973) and Sergey Brin (b. 1973) began to cooperate on developing a search engine they named BackRub, and they operated it on the Stanford University servers for almost twelve months. In 1997 the duo decided to rename the search engine and give it a more catchy title. They were looking for a word that represented an enormous figure and came upon the word "googol," which is written out as a "1" followed by a hundred zeros. They decided to use a play on the word and settled on "Google."

In September 1998 the company was set up in the garage of Susan Wojcicki in Menlo Park, California, and the two founders hired their first employee, Craig Silverstein, whom they knew from Stanford. After positive reviews in *PC Magazine* in 1998, they moved from their garage to offices in Palo Alto the following January. By June they had raised $25 million capital investment from Sequoia Capital and Kleiner Perkins.

In June 2000, Google became the world's biggest search engine, overtaking Yahoo! In December of the same year, they introduced their masterstroke, the Google toolbar, which, when installed on a computer, saves the need to visit the Google Web site to browse the web.

In August 2004, the stunning Google IPO (Initial Public Offering), raised over $1.6 billion in share capital to fund their next round of expansion.

In the third quarter of 2008, Google reported revenues of $5.54 billion. The company now employs over 20,000 people and has a market capitalization above $110 billion, having been valued at almost $200 billion before the bank crisis hit the world. By comparison, Yahoo's capitalization was $18 billion, Microsoft's was $200 billion, and Apple's was $95 billion. The computer company IBM, a business founded in 1889, was slightly ahead of Google at $124 billion.

In 2007, the sales came to $59 billion, and profit was $4.2 billion. The two founders came in at joint fifth among the richest Americans with $18.5 billion each. At that date their business was only eleven years old.

DUPONT

The du Pont family had a lucky escape from the mob during the French Revolution, and landed as refugees in America on January 1, 1800. Eleuthere (1771–1834), the second son, had studied gunpowder production under the famous French chemist Antoine Lavoisier. In 1802 he founded E. I. du Pont de Nemours in Brandywine Creek in Wilmington, Delaware, to manufacture black powder (gunpowder). By the middle of the nineteenth century, the company had become the biggest supplier of gunpowder to the United States Army.

DuPont describes itself nowadays as a global science company, and most of its products come from the application of scientific research. It offers a product line that includes such well-known brands as:

Cellophane, Nylon, Lucite, Neoprene, Mylar, Dacron, Lycra, Tyvek, Kevlar, Stainmaster, and Thermolite.

Sales in 2007 were $32.6 billion and profit was $3.0 billion.

MICROSOFT

Microsoft was founded in Albuquerque, New Mexico, in 1975 by William (Bill) H. Gates (b. 1955), and Paul G. Allen (b. 1953).

The founders realized that the future lay in producing operating systems for the rapidly emerging home computer market, rather than trying to compete with the likes of Apple, Commodore, and IBM in producing hardware. Continual upgrades would ensure their market was sustained.

The company rose to dominance of the home computer operating system market through the 1980s. The early MS-DOS system was followed by the Windows operating system in 1985, and it is estimated that Microsoft Windows now accounts for 90 percent of the world's computer operating system market.

> "I believe in the inexhaustible ability of human beings to find answers to problems."
> **—Paul Allen**

GENERAL ELECTRIC

GE was formed in 1892 in Schenectady, New York, by the merger of Edison Electric (founded by Thomas Alva Edison) and Thomson-Houston Electric.

The General Electric brand is the fourth most valuable in the world, with a dollar value of $49 billion. The company is regularly voted the "Most Admired" in *Fortune Magazine*.

In each divisions—including aviation, lighting, medical imaging, automation, finance, and health care—General Electric is either number one or number two in the world.

EXXON

Exxon is a brand of fuel sold by the Exxon-Mobil Corporation, the world's largest publicly traded oil company. Its products are sold in every country in the world. The company was formed in 1882 as Standard Oil of New Jersey, and was part of the immense Standard Oil Trust created by John D. Rockefeller (1839–1937). Rockefeller became the world's richest man and is often considered to have been, in relative terms, the richest man in history.

In 2007 Exxon-Mobil was the world's most profitable company with more than $40 billion in earnings.

And another thing . . .

The Esso brand came from the initials S-O of Standard Oil, but under U.S. legislation, the name and brands were changed in 1973 to Exxon.

WAL-MART

1962 was a watershed year in discount retailing. It saw the launch of K-Mart, Target, and Woolco. Wal-Mart was also born in 1962 and rose from its humble beginnings to dominate the world of retailing.

In 1962, Sam Walton invested heavily to open a single 16,000-square-foot store in Rogers, Arkansas. The store was an immediate success and customers encouraged Walton to open other stores. He looked around for a suitable opportunity and found a site in Harrison, Arkansas, where he opened his second store in 1964.

Launch day came close to disaster. Temperatures had risen to 115°F and hundreds of watermelons, which Walton had instructed his staff to stack outside, began to pop. Families had been encouraged to bring along their children for a free donkey ride, and the donkeys did what donkeys do, in the middle of the spilt melon juice. The customers walked through the resultant mess on the way from the parking lot, and trailed it into the store.

David D. Glass, the future chief executive of Wal-Mart, who was attending as the representative of another company at the time, records that he thought Sam Walton was probably a very nice man, but gave him no chance of making a success of retailing. Launch day had not been a success, but the store continued to offer discount prices for groceries, and the customers just kept pouring in.

Within sixteen years, Wal-Mart had opened 276 stores in eleven states and had sales of more than $1 billion. By 1990 there were 1,531 stores in twenty-nine states and sales above $25 billion.

Sam Walton died in 1992, but by then his "baby" had grown to become the largest retailer in the United States. As of 2000, the company had become by far the biggest retailer in the world, and the largest company of any type in the world by sales value. The payroll listed more than 1 million employees.

In 2007, Wal-Mart, which is still based in Bentonville, Arkansas, had retained its position as the biggest company of any sort in the world, with annual sales of almost $400 billion and more than 2 million employees.

BOEING

Boeing Corporation's aircraft fly to almost every country on Earth. It is the world's largest aircraft manufacturer, supplying its products to every national airline, and for several years it has been America's biggest exporter.

Its best-known brands are McDonnell Aircraft, Douglas Aircraft, and Hughes Helicopters. The ubiquitous Boeing 747, often referred to as the "Jumbo Jet," completed its first commercial flights in 1970 for Pan Am and TWA. It remains in production and is by far the most successful passenger aircraft ever built, with more than 1,400 having been in service at one time or another.

William Edward Boeing (1881–1956) was born in Detroit, Michigan, and after an early career in trading forestlands in Washington—the career that earned him his first fortune—he traveled to Los Angeles to attend the first aviation meeting ever held in the United States. Boeing was so taken with the spectacle of men in flying machines that he tried to persuade each of the dozen pilots taking part to take him aloft. They all refused.

Five years later, Boeing formed a partnership with George Conrad Westervelt to build better aircraft than any that were then available. Their first airplane, the Model C, was a float seaplane but did not sell well. After Westervelt left the company to return to the East Coast, Boeing was obliged to use his own money to guarantee the costs. The first production order for 334 of the Model C came from the U.S. military in 1918, late in World War I. The military planned to use them for pilot training, but the war ended within months and the company suddenly faced severe financial difficulty. It pulled through by diversifying into furniture manufacture as well as aircraft.

By the end of World War II, Boeing had established itself as a major aircraft producer and it went on to complete pioneering work in passenger jets, satellites, and lunar vehicles.

The company now has a key role in HiFire (Hypersonic International Flight Research Experimentation) for the U.S. Air Force Research Laboratory. HiFire is a program, in partnership with NASA and the Australian Defence Force, to test the latest technology in space launch vehicles and weapons. One of the experiments is to have HiFire test vehicles dive into the atmosphere at Mach 4 to 8 (between 4 and 8 times the speed of sound) to obtain data for hypersonic flight.

Sales in 2007 totaled $66.4 billion with profits of $4.1 billion.

PROCTER & GAMBLE

Procter & Gamble has a long history that begins with two men, William Procter (1801–1884), a candle maker, and James Gamble (1803–1891), a soap maker. They met because their respective wives were sisters. For years they competed for scarce resources for their individual businesses, which led to family tensions. Finally their shared father-in-law suggested that the two should go into business together. They formed Procter & Gamble in 1837 and continued to produce candles and soap. The business was an immediate success. In 1859, the company achieved its first year with annual sales of $1 million, which was an enormous sum at the time.

Procter & Gamble, based in Cincinnati, Ohio, sells its household consumables throughout the world. Its brands include Ariel washing powder, Gillette razors, Pantene hair treatment, Oral toothbrushes, Crest toothpaste, Head & Shoulders shampoo, Iams pet food, Tide laundry detergent, and Pringles snacks.

The group is credited with pioneering "brand management" and according to Nielson Media Research, it is by far the biggest spender on advertising in the world. In 2007 it spent $2.62 billion—twice as much as its nearest competitor.

P & G's first venture into overseas business came in 1930 with the acquisition of a well known candle- and soap-maker in England, the Thomas Hedley Company based in Newcastle-upon-Tyne.

In 2007 P & G's worldwide sales was $76 billion and they made a profit of $10.3 billion.

TUPPERWARE

In 1946, Earl Silas Tupper (1907–1983) developed a home products line of plastic containers that could be used for storage, serving, and preparation of foodstuffs.

Tupperware had two distinguishing features: the "burping seal" that keeps the container airtight, and the "Party Plan" method of marketing the range of products. Both of these features gave Tupper a distinct advantage over his competitors.

The Tupperware Party Plan strategy came from Brownie Wise, one of Tupper's distributors. The idea is for the sales agent to host parties in his or her home and display the wares in a relaxed atmosphere. The plan was to tap into the social network of each agent and for that agent to recruit more agents to do the same thing, creating a massive network of sales personnel throughout the country. Wise set up the corporate culture of Tupperware, and made sure the agents were highly incentivized with exotic prizes and trips.

In the 1950s and 1960s, Tupperware sales took off and the company soon began to cast its eyes on Europe. In 1960, the first overseas operation was set up in London, and nowadays Tupperware is sold in more than 100 countries.

Religions

BORN IN THE USA

O ne of the more important signs of a tolerant society is the extent to which that society allows freedom of worship.

Some countries allow only a single religion—the state religion. By that means, the state bureaucracy feels it is able to keep control over the fundamental thought processes of its citizens.

By contrast, the United States has a bewildering array of religions, several of which have been started just in the last century. Unlike many European countries, in which different religious practices are merely mild variations on Christianity, a different way of worshipping the same God, the United States seems to have fostered and tolerated new religions to suit all tastes, every possible prejudice, and new gods.

Here are the main ones.

NATION OF ISLAM

It is believed that the prophet Noble Drew Ali, born Timothy Drew (1886–1929) in North Carolina, was the son of slaves. In 1913, he founded the Moorish Science Temple of America in Newark, New Jersey, and although he was forced to flee, first to Philadelphia, and then to Chicago, by the late 1920s, Ali's church had around 15,000 followers.

The main tenet of the Moorish Science Temple is that African Americans are descended from the Moors, and are therefore originally Muslim.

Following Drew Ali's death in 1929, the church divided twice. One of the divisions was led by Wallace Fard Muhammad who set up the first mosque in Detroit in 1930. His disappearance in 1934 has remained a mystery, but the movement he led came to be known as the American Nation of Islam. The Nation of Islam varies in some respects to the traditional Islamic faith, but follows the "Five Pillars of Islam": prayer five times a day facing Mecca, charity to the poor, fasting during the holy month of Ramadan, pilgrimage to Mecca at least once in one's lifetime, and profession of the faith.

The adherents of Islam, known as Muslims (those who submit to the will of Allah), believe that Islam has always existed, but was revealed by degrees to ancient prophets. In Islam, God is Allah, and the theology of Islam allows no other belief.

In 610 CE the final revelation was made to the Prophet Mohammed (c. 570–632 CE) as he meditated alone in a cave. According to tradition, the Angel Jibreel (Gabriel) visited Mohammed and instructed him to recite the word of Allah. During the rest of his life he continued to receive revelations, which were written down as the Qu'ran (Koran).

The other holy book of Islam is the Hadith, which is an account of the spoken traditions attributed to the Prophet Mohammed. It is revered and received in Islam as a major source of religious law and moral guidance.

MORMONISM

Mormonism is more properly known as The Church of Jesus Christ of Latter-day Saints. The doctrine of the church holds that at some time after the events depicted in the New Testament, there was a Great Apostasy, or loss of authority to lead the Christian Church. It teaches that John the Baptist, James, John, and Peter visited the leaders of the Church in 1829 and gave them authority to reestablish the Church of Christ.

At the age of twenty-two in 1827, Joseph Smith (1805–1844) began to write the *Book of Mormon* and founded the Mormon faith. The *Book of Mormon* was completed in 1830 and contained more than 250,000 words (a typical novel contains about 70,000 words).

Smith preached widely and sold the *Book of Mormon* in large numbers so that the Mormon Church acquired many thousands of followers across America. Mormons regarded Joseph Smith as a latter-day prophet at least as important as Moses.

Brigham Young (1801–1877), who had joined Joseph Smith in 1833, took up the leadership of the Church after Smith's death, and in 1847 led the people to Salt Lake City, Utah. (At that time, Utah was in Mexico.)

The Church, which is based on Christianity, believes that God's revelations come through modern prophets such as Joseph Smith and Brigham Young, and that the Holy Trinity exists as three separate entities. Mormons abstain from caffeine, smoking, alcohol, and illegal drugs. Salt Lake City became to Mormonism what Rome is to Roman Catholicism, the de facto capital of the religion.

SCIENTOLOGY

The Church of Scientology began with a bestselling book called *Dianetics: The Modern Science of Mental Health*, written by American science-fiction writer L. Ron Hubbard (1911–1986) and published in May 1950. Hubbard, who is the founding father of Scientology, began preaching his first messages in Phoenix, Arizona, in the autumn of 1951, and by the spring of 1952 the new religion had more than 15,000 adherents. The first church of Scientology was built in Los Angeles in 1954.

Hubbard introduced Scientology as a study of knowledge. Its founding principles are a form of religious philosophy dedicated, through counseling, to the rehabilitation of the human spirit. The Church of Scientology holds that by personal observation and experience, individuals can discover for themselves whether Scientology works for them, without having to rely on blind belief. It also advocates that people are immortal spiritual beings, who live many lifetimes.

Hubbard continued to introduce fresh doctrines for the last thirty-four years of his life.

From its early days, Scientology and its leaders have faced prosecutions for tax evasion, charges of fraud, and accusations of conspiracy to steal government papers. The Church has also often been criticized for the financial demands it puts on its members, and for what are seen as bogus scientific and religious claims.

MOONIES

More properly known as the Unification Church, the Moonies were founded in Seoul, South Korea in 1954, by the Reverend Sun Moon (real name Yung Myung Moon) (b. 1920). But it was in the United States that the Moonies made their greatest advances.

In 1945, Moon wrote *The Divine Principles*, which became the scripture of the Moonies, but there is evidence to suggest that he stole many of his ideas and teachings from two other cults he had earlier been involved with. Moon's overriding claim is that when he was sixteen years old, Jesus came to him on a mountain in North Korea and asked him to fulfill his mission on Earth. The Unification Church holds many of the traditional Christian beliefs, but also believes that the death of Jesus was not preordained, and that in the Final Days, Satan will become a good angel. The Reverend Moon claims that he is the Messiah of the Second Coming.

Moon achieved success in his quest to build a new religion after the 1961 coup in South Korea, in which the military led by General Park Chung-hee (1917–1979) overthrew the civilian government. In 1971, after a couple of periods in jail on tax evasion charges, Moon moved his base to the USA, where the media named his followers Moonies, and it was here that the growth of the movement began.

The organization owns the *Washington Times* and hundreds of other businesses, including a firearms producer.

Music and

Dance

Modern American music and dance has had a powerful cultural effect on the rest of the world. No other country has "exported" its national musical cultures so successfully.

Perhaps opera, which began its life in Italy, is the only other music that left its cultural birthplace to migrate over the whole planet. The English Morris dance, the Irish jig, French accordion music, the wail of the Scottish bagpipe: they barely made it past customs. They remain fixed in their own backyard, and are not always popular there.

Through its accessibility and general feel-good factor, American music and dance has always appealed to the young, who take up new offerings en masse.

"If music be the food of love, play on."
(Twelfth Night)

—William Shakespeare

(1564-1616)

MUSIC

JAZZ

If it hadn't been for the American slave trade, it is hard to say whether jazz would have been born, either in Africa or America. Jazz expresses the music of the native African who has been isolated far from home.

West African tribal music had developed—in ways unknown to Westerners—through the use of voice and percussion, and early slave songs followed the same pattern. The slave songs served the function of maintaining work rates on the cotton plantations, railroads, and levees of the Deep South. The early work songs, particularly those of Leadbelly (real name Huddie Ledbetter) (1888–1949), survived long after their functional needs had declined.

In a strange twist of fate, missionaries who tried for years to convert slaves to Christianity succeeded in achieving the Africanization of their own hymnbooks through the introduction of new vocal styles and percussion.

Leadbelly

The spiritual was born out of revival chants, camp songs, and funeral music. This led to ragtime, the bridge between the old slave songs and the emerging jazz music. The direct connection with sacred music underlines the common fallacy that jazz emerged only from the lowlife, although it is true that the brothels of New Orleans provided many of the early jazz stars with the opportunity to develop their musical talents.

Jazz burst out of the United States and into the rest of the world during the late nineteenth century and early twentieth century. It continued to develop through Dixieland, Blues, the Big Band era, and Swing with an immense collection of virtuoso musicians such as Duke Ellington, Fats Waller, and Art Tatum.

It has never lost its appeal.

ROCK AND ROLL

In the early 1950s, rock and roll exploded out of America into the consciousness of the world. It evolved out of rhythm and blues, gospel, and country music, and is characterized by the use of amplified electric guitars, youth-oriented lyrics, and an insistent, heavily accented offbeat. No music had ever so completely captured the imagination of a whole generation.

There are a number of contenders for the accolade of the world's first rock-and-roll record. It is generally thought that "Rock Around the Clock" by the American group Bill Haley and the Comets was the first rock-and-roll record. It did enter the charts, but Haley (1925–1981) had scored an earlier success with "Shake, Rattle and Roll," which was released in April 1954 and sold 1 million copies. "Rock around the Clock" was also released in April 1954, but it only sold 75,000 copies on first release. It later became a worldwide hit after it was featured in *Blackboard Jungle*, a film released in late 1954. It was the first rock-and-roll record to top both the American and British charts. According to some authorities, worldwide record sales for "Rock Around The Clock" currently top 25 million.

Other sources regard Elvis Presley's (1935–1977) "That's All Right, Mama" as the first rock-and-roll record into the charts, but it was not released until July 1954, three months after Bill Haley's records.

Before Bill Haley formed his group in 1949 Jimmy Preston (1913–1984) released "We're Gonna Rock This Joint Tonight" in 1949. This record was also covered by Bill Haley and the Saddlemen in 1953, and is regarded as the prototype of rock-and-roll music, although some claim "Rocket 88 (written by Ike Turner)," released in 1951 by Haley, is the true prototype.

And another thing . . .

In 1922, blues singer Trixie Smith (1895–1943) recorded "My Daddy Rocks Me with a Steady Roll." This record has a strong claim to be the first use of the words "rock and roll" in popular music. In blues music, the words rock and roll were often used to refer to sexual intercourse.

PUNK ROCK

Punk rock began in the USA, not, as is widely believed, in Britain. The term "punk rock" was applied to untutored music with simplistic arrangements, and was coined by the U.S. music critic Dave Marsh in May 1971. Early exponents were The Ramones and The Sex Pistols (previously The Swankers), but by 1978 it was pretty much all over for punk.

GRAMOPHONE (a.k.a. RECORD PLAYER)

Thomas Alva Edison (1847–1931), the great American inventor, produced the forerunner of the gramophone, the phonograph, in 1877.

Emile Berliner (1851–1929), became an American citizen after emigrating from Germany at age nineteen. Berliner coined the word "gramophone" in 1894 as a trademark for his new and improved design of phonograph. Berliner's machine was the first to use flat discs in place of the cylinders that were used in phonographs.

JUKEBOX

The word "jukebox" may have derived from the Elizabethan English word *jouk*, meaning "to move quickly or dodge," or the African American slang term *jook*, meaning "to dance."

The first coin-operated machine to play recorded music was installed on November 23, 1889, by Louis Glass (1864–1936) in the Palais Royal Saloon in San Francisco. Glass linked an electrically operated Edison phonograph to four listening tubes, each of which was separately coin-operated. The well-known term "nickel in the slot machine" was coined to describe it.

The first jukebox, as we would recognize it today, was invented in 1905 by John C. Dunton of Grand Rapids, Michigan. The customer had a choice of twenty-four preselected recordings, each of which was on a wax cylinder.

After an initial boom in popularity, jukeboxes went into decline during the 1930s and 1940s. Demand was stimulated again after sound quality had been improved by better speaker technology. The advent of rock-and-roll music in the 1950s came along at precisely the right time to take advantage of the new jukeboxes.

ELECTRIC GUITAR

The electric guitar, with its unique soaring chords and its ability to tap directly into the psyche of the young, was crucial to the development of rock and pop music. Lloyd Loar of the USA developed the original prototype in 1924, and his first commercial model, the Vivi-Tone, was launched in 1933.

Despite the Vivi-Tone being a commercial flop, the electric guitar had established a foothold as the legitimate musical instrument for the youth of the world.

MOOG SYNTHESIZER

In 1964, Robert Moog (1934–2005), a U.S. engineer, invented his eponymous synthesizer in his Trumansburg, New York workshop. His revolutionary instrument was able to produce haunting musical notes entirely by electronic means. The first live performance was given in 1964. Moog developed his ideas from building Theremin electronic music kits at home. The theremin was an early electronic musical instrument invented by the Russian cellist Leon Theramin, which produced music by altering the sine curve in the sound wave. Moog sold around 1,000 of these before starting to make his own instruments, collaborating with two composers: Herbert Deutsch and Walter (later Wendy) Carlos (b. 1939).

After the success of Carlos's album *Switched-On Bach*, which was the first album produced using only electronic instruments, the Beatles and Rolling Stones bought synthesizers and the word "Moog" passed into pop legend.

And another thing . . .

"Moog" is one of the most mispronounced words in music. It should be pronounced to rhyme with "vogue."

HIT PARADE

The first sheet-music sales chart was topped by the Ink Spots in January 1950 with "You're Breaking My Heart."

The original number one in the U.S. *Billboard* magazine Hit Parade chart was "Wheel of Fortune," sung by Kay Starr (b. 1922) in March 1952.

In 1949, Todd Stortz (1924–1964) bought the ailing radio station KOWH in Omaha. In 1953 he revitalized its fortunes by converting the station to an all-hits type, and at the same time, he pioneered the format of having the Top 40 record hits, played on a countdown to number one. He blew away the competition, which only played the top twenty, beginning at number one.

DANCE

"A dance to the music of time."

—Anthony Powell (1905-2000)

OKEY COKEY or HOKEY POKEY

The okey cokey originated in Kentucky as a nineteenth-century Shaker song, with silly words, and an associated group dance. The dancers stand in a ring and sing: "You put your right arm in, you put your right arm out. You put your right arm in, and you shake it all about . . ." while doing exactly that. The okey cokey, like other dance crazes, was taken to Europe during World War II by American servicemen.

CHARLESTON

Among popular dances, the Charleston is perhaps the most difficult to master. The steps are characterized by rapid heels-out, toes-in twisting steps, and can be performed solo or with any number of partners at the same time. In its earliest form, the Charleston included complex rhythms that were beaten out with foot-stamping and hand claps.

It was first performed in 1903 in Charleston, South Carolina. By 1913 it had transferred to the stage in Harlem, New York, and in 1920, professional dancers had adopted it. The dance made its first appearance in a musical in *Runnin' Wild* in 1923.

By the 1930s, the Charleston was being performed all over the world.

BLACK BOTTOM

The black bottom was introduced in New Orleans in 1919 by song-writer Perry "Mule" Bradford (1893–1970) and the blues singer Alberta Hunter (1895–1984). Bradford claimed that he had seen a similar dance performed in 1907 called the Jacksonville Rounders Dance, which was not a success, as "rounder" is another word for "pimp."

The black bottom was a solo "challenge" dance, which featured slapping the backside while simultaneously hopping backwards and forwards and gyrating the hips. In 1926 the dance became the latest fashion on both sides of the Atlantic and began to replace the Charleston.

LINDY HOP

The Lindy Hop developed in 1927 in New York.

Around this time, a great many new dances began to emerge, such as the Texas Tommy, the Charleston, the Breakaway, the Grizzly Bear, and the Loving Hug. The Lindy Hop adopted many of the steps in these dances and blended them into a dance that traveled overseas to Europe and Asia.

The world's most famous person of the time was Charles Lindbergh (1902–1974) who was popularly known as Lucky Lindy. His fame and popularity came from completing the first solo, nonstop transatlantic flight from New York to Paris in 1926. Newspapers reported the event with headlines stating "Lindy Hops the Atlantic." In a 1927 dance marathon at the Manhattan Casino in Harlem, New York, one of the dancers, George (Shorty) Snowden, was asked what dance he was actually performing and he answered, "I'm doing the Lindy Hop," which is the first known reference. Lindy Hop was thereafter adopted as the name for the dance.

JITTERBUG

The jitterbug dance was created by the bandleader Cab Calloway (1907–1994), but the term "jitterbug" was actually coined in 1934 by Harry Alexander White. It was a popular, exuberant swing dance in the USA in the 1930s and 1940s and featured the dancers energetically swinging and twisting round each other, with plenty of hip and arm movement.

During World War II, 1.5 million American servicemen arrived in Britain, bringing the jitterbug with them. Horrified dance hall proprietors not used to seeing such energetic dances, and wanting to preserve their wooden dance floors, soon erected notices reading NO JITTERBUGGING. It had little effect and the jitterbug dance spread throughout Europe after the end of the war.

JIVE

Jive dance descended from jitterbug and country dancing in the USA. It has little connection with its predecessor, the Charleston, but the Lindy Hop and Jitterbug, with their exuberant twisting and spinning, are closely related.

Jive originated in the African American community in the 1940s and was brought to Europe by American soldiers. The young quickly adopted the new dance, and its popularity continued into the mid-1960s, with its close connection to rock-and-roll music.

In the elite world of ballroom dancing, jive is now designated as one of the five international "Latin" dances.

THE TWIST

The Twist was popularized as a dance craze in 1960, and went on to dominate dance halls, weddings, and club socials for more than a decade.

The song "Let's Twist Again" was written by Hank Ballard (1927–2003), who released it as a "B" side in 1959. However, it was the Carolina-born Chubby Checker (b. 1941) who scored hits all over the world with it, and in 1960, he topped the charts on both sides of the Atlantic. Chubby's great "sales pitch" was to open every performance with a simple dance lesson. He ensured his audience maintained the rhythm and activity by performing the steps of the twist as he sang. Critics felt that the dance itself was too sexually provocative, but the youth of the world quickly adopted the basic steps of the twist, and used them to accompany other dance tunes.

In 2008, *Billboard* magazine announced that Chubby Checker's "The Twist" was the biggest chart success of all time.

And another thing . . .

Chubby Checker's real name was Ernest Evans. His stage name was given to him by the wife of Dick Clark as a play on the name of jazz great Fats Domino (b. 1928).

Singers, Songwriters, and Musicians

The staple substance for singers of popular music is an American accent.

A strange phenomenon overcomes singers from non-American, English-speaking countries when they sing popular songs. They adopt an American accent. Some hardly know they're doing it, or if they do, why they're doing it, but they manage to stretch their vowels, make the "t" sound like "d" and use the same pauses as their American counterparts. Listen to Mick Jagger, Sting, or Freddie Mercury and you could be hearing a voice that grew up in the USA. Forget using clipped English vowels in pop, rock, country, or jazz. Anyone who tried it would be laughed off stage. One of the few times it's okay to use "English" English is in comic songs. Gilbert and Sullivan songs are a good example. They suit the English accent because they're creating a parody of the straitlaced English characters they're portraying.

Somehow, the passion, or the essential truth of an English language chart song is lost with Australian, English, Welsh, or Scottish accents. The Irish accent can just about work. Canadian counts as American for this purpose. The Beatles were an exception to this rule, as their songs were practically designed for the Liverpool accent.

The wonderful voices and creativity of the artists on the following pages have been the sound of America around the world. Whether they are heard on jukeboxes, iPods, or broadcast radio programs, this is what America sounds like to the rest of the world.

Some singers, such as Bob Dylan, are the voices of their generation. Others, like Johnny Cash and Tammy Wynette, are the voices of the human condition. Still others, like Fats Domino, sing about light and fancy things. All are unmistakeable.

When a Beatles song is played in public, listeners don't think "English," they think "Lennon and McCartney." On the other hand, when a song by Irving Berlin, Jerome Kern, Brian Wilson, or Bob Dylan is played in some far country, subconsciously the listener thinks "American."

America's singers (including some of the greatest opera stars in history), musicians, and songwriters have left their indelible stamp on the world's music wherever it's played.

LOUIS ARMSTRONG

Louis Armstrong (1901–1971) (a.k.a. Satchmo) was one of the all-time greats of jazz. He is without peer as the most famous jazz trumpeter in history, and the first great solo jazz performer to emerge in the twentieth century. As well as his virtuosity with the trumpet, his uniquely deep, rough-edged voice was—and remains—instantly recognizable, whether singing, speaking, or just laughing.

He was born into a poor family, the grandson of slaves, and had to work immensely hard right through his early life. His first job was newsboy and later, he hauled coal into the "red light" district of New Orleans to bring some money into his home. Just by living in New Orleans, Armstrong was exposed to a vast array of music and dance. This continuous exposure ignited in him the desire to play piano, but he migrated to trumpet at a later date. Through his musicianship, Armstrong became an immortal of the jazz world, and even today, nearly forty years after his death, Armstrong's music is heard and his voice is recognized all over the world.

JOAN BAEZ

Joan Chandos Baez (b. 1941) dealt with social issues in her songs. With her haunting voice and highly recognizable style of singing, she was prominent throughout the world during the 1960s. In 1957 she bought her first guitar, which was a Gibson. An aunt encouraged her to practice, and it was her aunt that had the notion that she should model her style of singing on Pete Seeger.

The professional career that Joan Baez had always craved began in earnest in 1959, when she performed at the Newport Folk Festival. She was instantly successful, and her next few albums all went gold in the charts.

In her songs she addressed many topical abuse issues such as human rights, gay and lesbian rights, the Vietnam War, the death penalty, and poverty. Her distinctive voice brought home, in a compelling way, the message that the people of the world should never close their eyes to the worst of the human condition.

In 1963, Baez gave enormous assistance to the future career of Bob Dylan when she invited him onstage at the Newport Folk Festival. They sang a duet, "With God on Our Side." Baez and Dylan became linked romantically, and often appeared onstage together.

BURT BACHARACH

Burt Bacharach (b. 1928) wrote many memorable songs during the 1960s and 1970s, seventy of which made the top 40 on the U.S.

charts. His music traveled well—for example, he had forty top-40 hits in the UK.

His best-known works include "Walk on By," "The Look of Love," "Anyone Who Had a Heart," "I Say a Little Prayer," "Twenty-Four Hours from Tulsa," and "Close to You." Many of the finest performers of the time recorded his songs, including Dionne Warwick, The Beatles, Aretha Franklin, and Gene Pitney.

Bacharach's music is characterized by unusual rhythms and changing meters. He introduced the use of the flugelhorn in his compositions, which was almost unheard of in popular music. His music is so deeply ingrained in popular music culture around the world that his compositions have become standards.

And another thing . . .

From 1965 to 1980, he was married to Hollywood star, Angie Dickinson.

SAMUEL BARBER

Samuel Osborne Barber (1910–1981) composed opera, piano, and choral music. His *Adagio for Strings*, composed at twenty-eight, places him among the best-known of American classical music composers. This piece is considered to be one of the masterworks of modern composition, and its haunting melody has been played at state funerals around the world, including that of Princess Diana. It has also been used in several movies. On classical music radio stations, Barber's Adagio is regularly voted by the public as the most popular piece of the year, and in a recent poll it was called "the single most powerful piece of music ever written."

Barber, born in Pennsylvania, developed an early interest in music. Like Mozart before him, he began composing at an early age. He was seven when he attempted his first composition, and he tried to write an opera at ten. During his career, experimental classical music was all the rage, but he reverted to the age of Mozart and Brahms to compose true classical music.

Some harsh criticism during his career led him to retire from the spotlight. However, he did continue to compose music, and his final work was the 1978 orchestral piece, *The Third Essay for Orchestra*. He completed this knowing he had cancer and had little time left.

COUNT BASIE

William James Basie (1904–1984) (a.k.a. Count Basie) led the Count Basie Orchestra for close to fifty years. It was the most enduring of the big bands, and in that time, he collaborated with many of the greatest musicians of the day and provided the platform for other musicians and singers to develop their solo careers. Ella Fitzgerald and Frank Sinatra both sang with Count Basie.

Basie toured his band around the world, introducing thousands of listeners to the Big Band sound. He also made some movie appearances, with his most memorable part being in the 1974 film *Blazing Saddles* as himself.

His signature tune, "One O'Clock Jump," is included in the Library of Congress National Recording Registry.

IRVING BERLIN

Irving Berlin (1888–1989) lived to 101, and never learned to read music at a professional level. This didn't stop him from composing more than 3,000 songs, some of which are among the most memorable ever written. Berlin's technique for writing a musical score was to hum or play it to a professional arranger. The arranger would then transcribe the tune onto the page. Berlin's first arranger, Alfred Doyle, who transcribed "Alexander's Ragtime Band," was paid fifty cents a page. Helmy Kresa did most of Berlin's transcriptions and served as his secretary and arranger for over sixty years. Berlin also tried a device known as a transcribing piano, which enabled him to play the notes and have the machine do the transcription. In 1973, he donated the machine to the Smithsonian Museum.

Berlin was actually born in present-day Belarus, but was brought to America at age five. He is included here as he spent ninety-six of his 101 years in the United States, and in that respect, the music he created was born in the USA.

Among his most popular works were "White Christmas," "Anything You Can Do," "There's No Business Like Show Business," "Alexander's Ragtime Band," and "God Bless America." Unlike many creative artists, who worry themselves to an early grave, Berlin died peacefully in his bed.

Asked where he thought Berlin's place would be in American music, Jerome Kern said, "Irving Berlin *is* American music."

And another thing . . .

During World War II, Irving Berlin was an accidental guest at one of Winston Churchill's gatherings for influential people. The misunderstanding happened in 1944, when Churchill's wife, Clementine, who was a fan of Irving Berlin's music, asked Winston if he would find time to thank him for his war work. She had in mind a handshake and a few words, but Churchill insisted instead that he should be invited to lunch. At the end of the meal, Churchill turned and said; "Now Mr. Berlin, what in your opinion is the likelihood of my dear friend, the president, being reelected for a fourth term?"

Berlin said he felt his great name would ensure victory.

Churchill then asked him when he thought the war would end, and Berlin replied, "Mr. Prime Minister, I shall tell my children and my grandchildren that Winston Churchill asked me that question."

Churchill had mistaken Irving Berlin for the Oxford intellectual, Isaiah Berlin, who was a British link man with America at the time. As Isaiah Berlin was based in Washington, Churchill had no idea what he looked like. Still confused, he then asked Berlin what he had written recently, referring to his dispatches from Washington. Berlin replied "White Christmas."

Talking to his friends afterward, Berlin said it had been a puzzling lunch, and he hadn't got on very well with the prime minister.

LEONARD BERNSTEIN

Leonard Bernstein (1918–1990) was a multi-Emmy-winning American conductor, composer, and author. He was the first conductor born and educated in the United States of America to receive worldwide acclaim.

Bernstein is one of the most influential figures in the history of American classical music. He is well known for his long conducting relationship with the New York Philharmonic and for his compositions, which include West Side Story, Candide, and On the Town. He inspired the careers of later generations of American musicians, and encouraged the work of American composers. His recording of "Rhapsody in Blue" by George Gershwin, using the full orchestra, is considered to be the definitive version.

And another thing . . .

As Leonard Bernstein's funeral wound its way through the streets of Manhattan, construction workers who were working on buildings along the route removed their hard hats, and, in a moving tribute to the man who helped to popularize classical music shouted, "Good-bye, Lenny."

CHUCK BERRY

Charles Edward Anderson Berry (b. 1926) (a.k.a. Chuck Berry) was one of the pioneers of rock-and-roll music. He was inducted into the Rock and Roll Hall of Fame on its opening in 1986, and was named number six in the top 100 rock guitarists of all time by *Rolling Stone* magazine. He was a strong influence on early rock-and-roll guitar techniques.

Unlike many American musicians who rise above a very poor background and a deprived childhood, Berry was raised in a middle-class family, but despite his background, at eighteen he was arrested for an armed robbery. He was released on his twenty-first birthday.

He held a number of jobs in the years after that, including janitor and assembly-line worker, and he even trained as a beautician. At the same time, he started to perform country music with local bands. His dramatic stage presence and highly skilled guitar riffs soon gained him popularity, and when the rock-and-roll bandwagon began to move, he rode it as one of its main pioneers.

He wrote "Sweet Little Sixteen," "Roll Over Beethoven," and "No Particular Place to Go," and other rock-and-roll chart hits in the 1950s. He had over a dozen chart hits and is still performing today.

GARTH BROOKS

Troyal Garth Brooks (b. 1962) is second only to the Beatles for album sales, with almost 70 million albums sold in the USA. According to the latest reports from the RIAA (Recording Industry Association of America) Brooks is the biggest-selling solo artist, surpassing Elvis Presley on a recount.

Garth Brooks is the only artist to have had seven albums debut at number one on the *Billboard* 200. He also had hit records and sellout tours in South America, Australia, New Zealand, and the UK, although some British pop stations could hardly bring themselves to acknowledge his popularity.

At the peak of his fame around the world, Brooks retired from live performing in 2001 for family reasons, and now dedicates a large part of his time to charity work.

MARIA CALLAS

Sophia Cecelia Kalos (1923–1977), better known as Maria Callas, was born in Manhattan to Greek parents. Her voice, above all other opera voices, is instantly recognizable. She was the most renowned opera singer of the twentieth century and is known among the aficionados of opera simply as La Divina.

Much of Callas's life was spent trying to avoid scandal, but newspapers were only too happy to report her temperamental behavior, her tempestuous affair with Aristotle Onassis, the Greek ship owner, and her long rivalry with other singers. The publicity she generated undoubtedly added to her box-office appeal, and she filled every seat in every opera house she ever sang in.

The world of opera appears to outsiders as stuffy and straitlaced. Callas brought to this conservative world compelling onstage drama, especially in the great tragedy roles. The characters she portrayed were instantly believable in their grief. Her portrayal of Tosca in the 1965 production at the Royal Opera House in London defined the role. The production was designed by Franco Zeffirelli and the part of Scarpia was taken by Tito Gobbi. All future Toscas would be judged against Callas's sublime performance.

The great Italian conductor Carlo Maria Giulini said of Callas, "It is very difficult to speak of the voice of Maria Callas. Her voice was a very special instrument. The sound has a magical quality."

HOAGY CARMICHAEL

Howard Hoagland Carmichael (1899–1981) composed some of the best-known songs in history. His most famous songs are "Stardust," "Up a Lazy River," "Georgia on My Mind," and "I Get Along Without You Very Well (Except Sometimes)." He won his first Academy Award with "In the Cool Cool Cool of the Evening."

He was described in Alec Wilder's study of American music as the most talented, inventive, and sophisticated of the hundreds of writers composing pop songs in the first half of the twentieth century. As well as songwriting and singing, Carmichael appeared in fourteen Hollywood films, always playing one of his own songs.

And another thing . . .

In the book *Casino Royale*, Ian Fleming describes James Bond as "looking like Hoagy Carmichael but with a scar down one cheek."

JOHNNY CASH

Johnny Cash (1932–2003) sold over 90 million albums and wrote or cowrote many of the most memorable songs of the last fifty years.

Among his best-known songs are "Ring of Fire," "I Walk the Line," "A Boy Named Sue," and "Folsom Prison Blues."

Cash's recording career began in 1955, at the same time that he was holding down a job as an electrical appliance salesman. His first recorded song was "Hey Porter." It was produced at the Sun Recording studio under its formidable boss, Sam Phillips. (Phillips is notable as the discoverer of Elvis Presley.)

Johnny Cash

Cash's brand of American music and his truthful portrayal of the underdog, down on his luck and battling through adversity, struck a deep chord with a wide range of listeners throughout the world.

RAY CHARLES

Ray Charles Robinson (1930–2004) helped to shape the sound of rhythm-and-blues music. With his soulful voice, he delivered definitive versions of such standards as "America the Beautiful," "Hit the Road Jack," "What'd I Say?" and "Georgia on My Mind."

Charles was number two in *Rolling Stone* magazine's list of the 100 greatest singers of all time, behind only Aretha Franklin.

He began recording in 1947 and had his first hit with "Confession Blues," which hit number two on the R & B charts in 1949. At the end of his career, he sang duets with many of the top artists of the day, such as B. B. King, Van Morrison, and Gladys Knight, and influenced the performances of others such as Elton John and Willie Nelson. In 2004, actor Jamie Foxx won the Academy Award for Best Actor, portraying Ray Charles in the film *Ray*, the Hollywood biopic of his life.

NAT "KING" COLE

Nathaniel Adams Coles (1919–1965) remains almost as popular forty years after his death as when he was performing. His soft, exquisitely modulated, baritone voice was the main instrument that created his worldwide fame, even though he had established himself as a highly accomplished pianist before he began to record vocals.

He studied classical piano and could play anything from Bach to Rachmaninov. He was influenced by Earl Hines and was himself the inspiration for such luminaries as Bo Diddley, Art Tatum, and Errol Garner. He succumbed to lung cancer at the tragically early age of forty-five, but left a legacy of music that is as strong as ever.

AARON COPLAND

Aaron Copland (1900–1990) wrote "Fanfare for the Common Man," one of the most recognizable pieces of classical composition written in the twentieth century. It has been used as an introduction piece for Rolling Stones and Bob Dylan concerts, as theme music in TV programs and films, and as the wake-up call on November 19, 2008, for the crew on board Space Shuttle STS-126.

Copland was a prolific composer of concert, theater, ballet, and film music, managing to achieve a balance between the styles of modern music and traditional American folk music. The "Hoe Down" in his ballet *Rodeo* is one of the most compulsively "toe-tapping" pieces of classical music ever written.

He had a vast influence on American music and some of his notable students include Michael Tilson Thomas and Elmer Bernstein.

JOHN DENVER

Henry John Deutschendorf, Jr. (1943–1997), better known as John Denver, was one of the most popular artists of the 1970s. He performed American country music and wrote many of the songs he performed.

Among his most popular compositions are "Leaving on a Jet Plane," "Take Me Home, Country Roads," "Rocky Mountain High," and "Annie's Song."

Denver had a distinctive image. His longish blond hair, cut in a Dutch-boy style, was complemented by bell-bottom jeans and cowboy boots. His happy, positive image and his Western accent helped to create a warm feeling in his fans. In 1982, he had his hair cut short, and assumed a more sober and socially conscious image. His interests started to go beyond his music, and Denver began to promote some of his political and social ideals, and to undertake humanitarian work.

He lost his life in an aircraft crash, flying solo. Shortly after takeoff at Monterey Peninsular Airport, he lost control of the plane and crashed just off the coast.

BOB DYLAN

Robert Allen Zimmerman (b. 1941) is better known by his stage name, Bob Dylan. He toyed with several alternative stage names but claims the "D" sound in Dylan came on strongest.

Dylan has been a major figure in American music for over half a century, with such seminal works as "Blowin' in the Wind," "The Times They Are a-Changin'," "Mr. Tambourine Man," "Like a Rolling Stone," and "Lay Lady Lay." The 1960s was a decade of protest songs and Dylan's repertoire was among the most powerful of that era. What distinguished his compositions from the many others was the strong poetic line that ran through them.

He was influenced early in his career by the works of Woody Guthrie, and in turn, Dylan himself was an influence for many others such as The Beatles; Peter, Paul & Mary; Joan Baez; and even the Beat poet, Allen Ginsberg.

Dylan's voice was nasal, slightly "whiny," and not always in perfect tune, but when he sang the words of his own songs the effect was like gasoline on a fire. He electrified the rock-and-roll generation with his truthfulness, and used music to challenge the status quo. It is said that Dylan was the voice of the 1960s, and his early work remains a potent force despite the passage of over forty years.

DUKE ELLINGTON

Edward Kennedy Ellington (1899–1974) was one of the most influential figures in American music, and perhaps the best-loved. At the age of seven, he began piano lessons with the exotically named Mrs. Marietta Clinkscales. At first he felt more attracted to baseball than to music, but at age fourteen listened to some poolroom pianists in Washington, D.C., and it sparked his desire to improve his playing. He started to take his lessons seriously.

In 1917, he launched his professional musical career, and at his first booking, took home a meager seventy-five cents. Fortunately, his career took off after that disappointing start.

Through the 1930s, '40s, and '50s, Ellington, who always conducted his band from the piano, enjoyed a string of successes with a few minor career slumps in the middle. The slumps were generally caused by personal problems, not lack of popularity. In 1956, he appeared at the Newport Jazz Festival, and this successfully introduced him to a wider and younger audience. He continued to flourish, and in 1965 was nominated for the Pulitzer Prize for Music, but didn't win it. With his trademark elegance and humor, he said on hearing the news, "Fate is being kind to me. Fate doesn't want me to be famous too young." At the time, he was sixty-seven years old and at the pinnacle of the music world.

At the age of seventy-five, Duke Ellington died of lung cancer and pneumonia. He was interred at the Woodlawn Cemetery in the Bronx.

Twelve thousand people attended the funeral of this true great of the music world.

EVERLY BROTHERS

Don Everly (b. 1937) and his brother Phil (b. 1939) were top-selling artists worldwide during the great rock-and-roll era between 1957 and 1964.

Their close harmony–singing was instantly recognizable, and their first million-seller was only their second record, "Bye Bye Love," which topped the charts on both sides of the Atlantic.

Other notable successes were "Wake Up Little Susie" (1957), "All I Have To Do Is Dream" (1958), "Bird Dog" (1958), and "Cathy's Clown" (1960).

In 1986, the Everly Brothers were among the first ten inductees into the Rock and Roll Hall of Fame. Their music has influenced the Bee Gees, Simon and Garfunkel, and Paul McCartney.

ELLA FITZGERALD

Ella Jane Fitzgerald (1917–1996) is widely considered to be one of the great singers of the twentieth century. Her vocal range spanned three octaves, and the notes she hit were always pure. Her phrasing was impeccable, and she could equally sing jazz standards, pop songs, and ballads.

At various stages of her career, Fitzgerald collaborated with Louis Armstrong, Count Basie, and Duke Ellington. Sadly, toward the end of her life, she lost her sight and both legs to complications from diabetes.

TENNESSEE ERNIE FORD

Ernest Jennings Ford (1919–1991) was born and grew up in the state he adopted for his stage name, Tennessee. In 1939, he began his show business career as a radio announcer at his local station, WOPI in Bristol.

Ford became a first lieutenant in World War II and served on B29 bombers as a bombardier.

After the end of the war, he appeared regularly on radio and TV, and in 1955 scored a massive worldwide hit with the iconic "Sixteen Tons." The words, which were the lament of a coal miner, were in stark contrast to the standard, sugary fare of the pop music of the time. The song was ten weeks at number one in the country music charts and eight at number one in the pop charts.

ARETHA FRANKLIN

Aretha Louise Franklin (b. 1942) remains one of the great singer/songwriters of American R & B and soul music. To fans, she is simply The Queen of Soul.

In 2008, she was ranked number one in the *Rolling Stone* magazine list of the greatest singers of all time.

Franklin, who was the daughter of a Baptist minister, was a child prodigy, and signed her first recording contract at fourteen. By the end of the 1960s, she had had a string of major hits and in 1972, with sales of more than 2 million, *Amazing Grace* became the biggest-selling gospel album of all time.

Aretha Franklin continues to perform live concerts and record solo albums. The best singers of several generations have queued to sing duets with her, including Frank Sinatra, Mariah Carey, Whitney Houston, Annie Lennox, and Christina Aguilera. She has won Grammy awards in five decades—1960s, 1970s, 1980s, 1990s, and 2000s—and has influenced other singers for over forty years. Adding to her legendary status, in 2009 Aretha Franklin was chosen to sing "My country, 'Tis of Thee" at president Obama's inauguration.

JUDY GARLAND

Frances Ethel Gumm (1922–1969) (better known as Judy Garland) had a singing career that spanned almost the whole of her life. Her first stage appearance was at age two-and-a-half singing "Jingle Bells."

In 1929, she appeared in a Vitaphone "short" (a short film) singing with her sister. She went on to star as Dorothy Gale in *The Wizard of Oz* in 1939, and in 1940, she was awarded the Academy Juvenile Award for her part.

Her legacy has endured long after her death, with "Over the Rainbow" being ranked the number-one movie song of all time by the American Film Institute.

BOBBIE GENTRY

Roberta Lee Streeter (b. 1944) is known worldwide as Bobbie Gentry. She was one of the first female singers to write her own material. In 1967, she had her first hit single with "Ode to Billie Joe," which sold over 3 million copies worldwide. It proved to be her biggest-selling record and is still on the airwaves.

Gentry's later albums never matched the success of her first, although she collaborated with Glenn Campbell on a couple of them. She continued to record albums until 1978, when she retired from the music world and public life. A certain amount of mystery surrounds Bobbie Gentry's life since her retirement. Little is known about it except that she is thought to live in Los Angeles.

GEORGE and IRA GERSHWIN

George (1898–1937) and Ira (1896–1983) Gershwin collaborated to create some of the most memorable songs of the twentieth century. George composed the music, and Ira wrote the lyrics for more than a dozen Broadway shows and the opera *Porgy and Bess.*

Featured in the shows were numbers such as "I Got Rhythm," "Someone to Watch over Me," "Summertime," and "Embraceable You."

George died tragically young, but Ira continued writing and collaborated with other composers to bring about important changes in American music. In contrast to standard sugary offerings, his lyrics were witty and smart and used vernacular language, so that everyone could understand and relate to them.

George composed music for television and film, and also for the classical concert hall. Dozens of great singers have recorded his music, including Ella Fitzgerald, Louis Armstrong, Judy Garland, and Kate Bush. His musical *Of Thee I Sing* was the first musical to win a coveted Pulitzer Prize. At the age of thirty-eight, George died from a malignant brain tumor, which, it was thought, could have been caused by a blow from a golf ball when he was very young.

In 2007, the Library of Congress created the Gershwin Prize for Popular Song, naming the prize in honor of the Gershwin brothers. The prize is awarded annually "in recognition of the profound and positive effect of popular music on culture." The first recipient was Paul Simon.

The music of George and Ira Gershwin runs deep in the American consciousness and has been willingly adopted by the rest of the world.

WOODY GUTHRIE

Woodrow Wilson Guthrie (1912–1967) wrote hundreds of songs including "This Land is Your Land," which is archived in the U.S. Library of Congress.

He grew up in Okemah, Oklahoma. His mother was institutionalized when he was only fourteen and with his father absent on business in Texas, he was forced to work odd jobs to bring money in. It was during this time that Guthrie learned to play harmonica and began his climb toward stardom.

During the Great Depression of the early 1930s, Guthrie joined the migration of "Okies" toward California, leaving behind a young wife and three children. The basis for many of his songs was formed in this period. The songs are concerned with conditions faced by working-class people. He traveled the country, settling for a time in New York and later in Washington, where he began to sing peace songs, and then to live on Coney Island. His time on Coney Island was his most productive, in terms of writing.

Guthrie's music and the themes he addressed influenced later generations of singer/songwriters such as Bob Dylan; Pete Seeger; Bruce Springsteen; and the Scottish folksinger, Donovan.

In the final years of his life, Woody Guthrie suffered increasingly from the effects of Huntington's disease, a genetic disorder characterized by jerky and uncoordinated bodily movements. He fought it with great bravery, but the disease finally claimed him at the age of fifty-five.

BILLIE HOLIDAY

Billie Holiday (1915–1959), born Eleanora Fagan, wrote one of the great jazz classics, "Lady Sings the Blues," but is much better known for her wonderful singing. Perhaps the most important recording she made, which stayed in her repertoire for more than twenty years, was "Strange Fruit." Her recording is listed in the National Recording Registry of the Library of Congress. The words of the song addressed the issue of the lynching of African Americans in the Deep South, and Holiday claimed they reminded her of the death of her own father.

Holiday had a very distinctive way of delivering a song, which made her instantly recognizable then and now.

In 1972, Diana Ross (b. 1944) was cast as Billie Holiday in *Lady Sings the Blues*, a portrayal of her life.

BUDDY HOLLY

Charles Hardin Holley (1936–1959) was one of the great pioneers of rock-and-roll music. The music critic Bruce Eder described him as "the single most influential creative force in early Rock and Roll."

In 1957, Holly was catapulted to stardom when his first record, "That'll be the Day"—recorded with his band, The Crickets—shot to number one in singles charts all over the world. He followed this with a prolific writing and recording schedule and released "Words of Love," "Everyday," "Peggy Sue," "Oh Boy," "Rave On," "Heartbeat," and "Maybe Baby" over the following few months. He recorded "It Doesn't Matter Anymore" in early 1959, and later that year died in a plane crash in poor weather on the way to his next show. Two other top artists died on the same flight, Ritchie Valens and J. P. "The Big Bopper" Richardson.

Despite his tragically short life and career, in 2004, *Rolling Stone* magazine ranked Buddy Holly as thirteenth on its list of the most influential rock-and-roll artists of all time. He was the first and most distinctive user of the hiccupping "glottal stop" within the lyrics. It can be heard in the opening line of "Rave On": "Weh-eh-heh-eh-hell, little things you say and do, make me want to be with yuh-eh-hoo."

And another thing . . .

The Beatles are said to have adopted their name in reference to Holly's group, The Crickets.

SCOTT JOPLIN

Scott Joplin (1867/8–1917) is considered to be the most important composer of classic ragtime music. He is the best known of the early performers, and more than half a century after his death, his music enjoyed a significant revival when his composition "The Entertainer," was featured in the 1973 movie *The Sting*. The tune reached number three on the *Billboard* Hot 100 in 1974.

In his personal life, Joplin was quiet and slightly withdrawn, a major contrast to his exuberant and joyful musical compositions. He was a dignified and elegant man, and a little-known fact about Joplin outside the USA is that along with his earliest work, "Maple Leaf Rag," he composed several African American ballets. The first was called the *Ragtime Dance* and the next was *The Guest of Honor*. *The Guest of Honor* commemorated the historic dinner when Booker T. Washington was the personal guest of U.S. president Theodore Roosevelt—the first time an African American had dined in the White House. It had always been Joplin's ambition to raise ragtime to the level of classical music.

Joplin contracted syphilis, which took his life as America was about to enter World War I.

JEROME KERN

Jerome David Kern (1885–1945) wrote more than 700 songs. From this large output came classics such as "Ol' Man River," "Smoke Gets in your Eyes," "The Way You Look Tonight," and "A Fine Romance."

Beginning around 1902, Kern composed popular music and worked on Broadway. He became an early composer for Hollywood, and in 1915 and 1916 he supplied music for a sixteen-part film serial, *Gloria's Romance*. Those films are now lost. During the 1920s, Kern wrote a new musical every year, including the iconic *Show Boat* in 1927, in which he cooperated with Oscar Hammerstein. He continued to work at a high pitch for Hollywood and Broadway during the 1930s but after a heart attack in 1939, his doctors advised him to stop writing for Broadway (which was more stressful than writing for film).

Oscar Hammerstein was at Kern's side as he lay in the hospital from a cerebral hemorrhage. His favorite song was "I've Told Ev'ry Little Star," and when Hammerstein hummed the tune into his ear and received no response, he knew Kern had died.

And another thing . . .

Jerome Kern was named after Jerome Park, one of his parents' favorite places. The park was named after Leonard Jerome, the father of Jennie Jerome, the mother of British Prime Minister Winston Churchill.

MARIO LANZA

Alfredo Arnold Cocozza (1921–1959), known professionally as Mario Lanza, was one of the most naturally talented tenors of all time. He introduced an emotional depth to operatic arias that brought instant appeal to the general public, and it didn't hurt his career that he was also better-looking than most Hollywood stars of the time.

In 1951, Lanza portrayed Enrico Caruso in the film *The Great Caruso*. The movie was a smash hit around the world and was an immense stimulus to Lanza's career. Thirty-six years after the film's release, Caruso's son, writing in his biography of his father, heaped praise on Lanza's portrayal, saying, "I can think of no other tenor, before or since Mario Lanza, who could have risen with comparable success to the challenge of playing Caruso in a screen biography."

Lanza was publicly humiliated when he was dismissed from the set of *The Student Prince* in 1952 after enormous weight gains. With his self-confidence badly undermined, he quickly descended into years of alcohol abuse and eating binges. In 1959 he had a heart attack and developed double pneumonia, and later that year, in Rome, he died from a pulmonary embolism at only thirty-eight. The legacy he leaves is the influence his dramatic performance style had on later opera stars such as Placido Domingo, José Carreras, and Luciano Pavarotti.

BRENDA LEE

Brenda Lee (b. 1944) began her performing career at eleven, and in the 1960s, one of the greatest rock and pop music eras, only The Beatles, Elvis Presley, and Ray Charles sold more records. Despite her diminutive stature, she had a powerful voice. Her main hits were "Rockin' Around the Christmas Tree" and "I'm Sorry."

And another thing . . .

The opening act on Brenda Lee's 1962 UK tour was the then almost unknown Liverpool group, The Beatles.

LERNER AND LOEWE

Alan Jay Lerner (1918–1986) and Frederick Loewe (1901–1988) cooperated to write *Brigadoon* in 1947. Shortly after this major success, Loewe is known to have commented that he would never write with Lerner again. He was wrong.

Something happened to rekindle their partnership and they went on to cowrite *Paint Your Wagon* (1951), *My Fair Lady* (1956), *Gigi* (1958), and *Camelot* (1960).

All these shows transferred to the big screen and are still seen in reruns by millions every year.

JERRY LEE LEWIS

Jerry Lee Lewis (b. 1935) was one of the pioneers, and an immortal, of rock and roll. He brought the same sort of exuberance to his stage act as Little Richard. In 1957 he had major hits with "Great Balls of Fire" and "Whole Lotta Shakin' Goin' On."

At the age of twenty-three, Lewis married his third wife, who also happened to be his cousin. She was only thirteen years old at the time, and the marriage caused a great scandal. The British press exposed the details when the couple arrived in London, and a planned concert tour of England was canceled as a result. He dropped out of the music scene and it was 1961 before he made another recording, "What'd I Say," which he cut in the new Sam Phillips studio in Memphis.

In October 2008, fifty years after the scandal that damaged his career, Jerry Lee Lewis returned to England and appeared at two shows in London.

LITTLE RICHARD

The Reverend Richard Wayne Penniman (b. 1932), better known as Little Richard, was a key figure in the transition of rhythm-and-blues music to rock and roll. His early hits, "Good Golly Miss Molly," "Tutti Frutti," and "Long Tall Sally" exploded onto an unprepared public in the mid-1950s. His superdynamic "shouting" style of singing defined popular music's massive potential, and lit the fuse for other performers like Jerry Lee Lewis.

Jimi Hendrix said, "I want to do with my guitar what Little Richard does with his voice." The list of artists who cite Richard as a major influence on their music reads like the whole of the Rock and Roll Hall of Fame, from Otis Redding to David Bowie.

At the height of his fame in 1957, he stopped recording and turned toward his calling, evangelism, to enter the ministry.

GLENN MILLER

Alton Glenn Miller (1904–1944) was the best-known big band leader of the "swing" era. What distinguished his band from other major bands of the day was the "Miller sound," which he developed over several years. The orchestra lineup of five saxophones, four trumpets, four trombones, and three rhythm instruments produced a unique sound that is instantly recognizable as Glenn Miller music. The sound itself is difficult to describe, but the music it produces has an unusual "human" quality.

The best-known songs of the band's repertoire of the 1940s are "In The Mood," "Tuxedo Junction," "Chattanooga Choo Choo," and "Moonlight Serenade."

During World War II, when Glenn Miller was at the peak of his popularity, he decided to serve the war effort by joining up. He enlisted in 1942 and was placed in charge of an army band. On December 15, 1944, Major Glenn Miller decided to fly from London to Paris to entertain the troops. His aircraft was lost over the English Channel and Miller's remains were never found.

And another thing . . .

In World War II, General Jimmy Doolittle said of Glenn Miller that, next to a letter from home, he was the greatest morale booster in the European Theater of War. (Jimmy Doolittle is famous as the first pilot to achieve the aerobatic maneuver known as an "outside loop," that is a loop with the cockpit on the outside.)

ROY ORBISON

Roy Kelton Orbison (1936–1988) was a pioneer of rock and roll. He had one of the most distinctive voices in music, and could jump three octaves with what seemed like little effort. His recording career began in the 1950s but he had to wait until 1960 for his debut single the hit Parade. In that year, "Only the Lonely" made number one in the UK and number two in the U.S. Hot 100.

For the next three years, Orbison made several chart hits but was without a number one. Then came the big breakthrough in 1964. He released *Pretty Woman*, which went on to hit the number-one spot across the globe. The Roy Orbison legend was born.

The 1970s were not fruitful in terms of chart successes, but Orbison enjoyed something of a revival during the 1980s, collaborating with Bruce Springsteen and Bob Dylan in the band The Traveling Wilburys.

Roy Orbison suffered almost unendurable tragedy in his life. In 1966, his first wife, Claudette, was killed in a motorcycle accident and in 1968 he lost two of his three sons in a house fire. In 1988, he collapsed and died from a massive heart attack while he was visiting a friend.

The musical legacy he leaves is the recording of one of the purest voices to grace the popular music world. Bob Dylan said, "Roy was an opera singer. He had the greatest voice of all."

DOLLY PARTON

Dolly Rebecca Parton (b. 1946) is one of America's most successful country music recording artists, with twenty-six number-one hits. As proof of her enduring popularity, she has had top-40 hits in each of the last five decades. Her fame has spread all over the world.

Her voice is a distinctive soprano, which, combined with her voluptuous figure and flamboyant dress sense, creates a lasting impression, especially onstage.

Parton came from a deprived background and began performing for audiences as a child. At age nine, she appeared on radio shows and landed her first recording contract at thirteen.

She wrote many hit songs, including the immensely popular "I Will Always Love You." In 1974, she went to number one on the country charts with this song and Elvis Presley said that he liked it so much that he wanted to also record it. Presley's manager, the ever-demanding "Colonel" Tom Parker stated that he wanted half the publishing rights if Elvis recorded the song. However, Dolly Parton was not known as "The Iron Butterfly" for nothing. She refused point-blank, and claimed later that the royalties she received as a result of that decision alone would have allowed her to buy Graceland.

She has written several classics, among them "Jolene," and in 2001 was inducted into the Songwriters Hall of Fame.

ELVIS PRESLEY

Elvis Aaron Presley (1935–1977) acquired such fame throughout the world that he is one of the very few people who can be referred to simply by their Christian name. He is also known as "the King" and he has become, even thirty years after his premature death, a cultural icon not only in the USA but also in most other countries.

He had a hugely successful rock-and-roll career, beginning right at its birth. He blurred the edges between so-called black rhythm and blues and white country music. His uninhibited stage performances drove audiences of both sexes to a frenzy of excitement.

Elvis's first record was "That's All Right, Mama," which was released in 1954. It was the second rock-and-roll record ever released. He followed this with a seemingly endless stream of hits including "Heartbreak Hotel," "Hound Dog," "Blue Suede Shoes," and "Love Me Tender." His final tally of number-one hits stands at eighteen, which has been equaled (by Mariah Carey) but never surpassed. Even while serving in the U.S. Army, Elvis had a couple of number-one hits with "Hard Headed Woman" and "A Big Hunk O'Love."

Elvis was in poor physical condition when he died. He collapsed on his bathroom floor, possibly from anaphylactic shock caused by drug abuse. He was so much a part of the culture of the world that U.S. president Jimmy Carter was moved to issue a statement from the White House.

RODGERS AND HAMMERSTEIN

Richard Rodgers (1902–1979) and Oscar Hammerstein (1895–1960) were song-writing partners in the golden era of Broadway musicals. Their work not only appealed to a great many people but also, in a subtle way, addressed important social issues of the day. In works such as *South Pacific*, they clearly focus on the effects of racism, and in *The King and I* they highlight the issue of female slavery. Despite most of their songs having happy-go-lucky tunes, there are many examples of them weaving social themes into the lyrics.

Their most notable works are *Carousel, Oklahoma, The King and I, The Sound of Music*, and *The Flower Drum Song*. All of these shows are still running somewhere in the world, more than fifty years since the death of Oscar Hammerstein.

SIMON AND GARFUNKEL

Paul Simon and Art Garfunkel (both b. 1941) were among the most popular recording artists of the 1960s and 1970s. Their worldwide masterpiece album, *Bridge Over Troubled Water*, featured some seminal works such as "Mrs. Robinson," "The Sound of Silence," "The Boxer," and the title song, "Bridge over Troubled Water." The soundtrack of the 1967 film *The Graduate* was comprised entirely of Simon and Garfunkel songs.

Both artists now follow separate careers, with occasional reunions, usually to sellout crowds.

FRANK SINATRA

Francis Albert Sinatra (1915–1998) was a top singing star for over sixty years, a testimony to his enduring talent. He began recording in 1935 with The Three Flashes, who renamed themselves The Hoboken Four after Sinatra joined.

In 1971, he announced his retirement in suitably dramatic style. At the end of a concert in Hollywood, he left the stage with the words, "Excuse me while I disappear." He did not reappear for his usual encore. In 1973, he came out of retirement and performed for several years across the globe. His 1993 recording of "I've Got You Under My Skin," which he duetted with Bono, sold 2 million copies and went to number 3 on the *Billboard* chart.

At the Frank Sinatra Desert Classic golf tournament in 1994, Sinatra sang before a live audience for the final time, and in a touching sign-off, his last song was "The Best Is Yet to Come." Sinatra was often referred to as "Ol' Blue Eyes," and to mark his eightieth birthday, the Empire

State Building—the symbol of much that is great about the United States of America—switched on all its lights and glowed blue.

BRUCE SPRINGSTEEN

Bruce Frederick Joseph Springsteen (b. 1949) is known to his legions of fans simply as The Boss.

He has sold more than 120 million albums worldwide, evidence of his strong global fan base.

Bruce Springsteen

In 1965 at age sixteen, he became the singer and lead guitarist of the Castiles, a New Jersey rock band, but it would be 1973 before he became commercially viable.

Springsteen displays his American sentiments in the music he performs. In his two most famous albums, *Born to Run* (1975) and *Born in the U.S.A.* (1984) he shows his feelings for the glory of the everyday struggles in daily life. He is known for his strong political beliefs and for his support for the rebuilding efforts following the tragedy of September 11, 2001.

His songs have been chart successes for such diverse artists as Manfred Mann's Earth Band, Patti Smith, and the Pointer Sisters.

In 1984, Bruce Springsteen released the iconic single, "Born in the U.S.A." He wrote the song in 1981 and included it on the 1984 album of the same name. In 1984–1985, Springsteen generally opened his concerts with "Born in the U.S.A." and it never failed to rouse the audience to fever pitch.

Although the lyrics reflect American blue-collar values and the Vietnam War, they found sympathy around the world, and the song became one of the decade's major hits.

BRIAN WILSON

Brian Douglas Wilson (b. 1942) created the immediately recognizable sound of the Beach Boys. Together with Mike Love, Wilson wrote the 1960s hits "Surfin' USA," "Fun Fun Fun," "God Only Knows," "California Girls," "Wouldn't It Be Nice," and "Good Vibrations."

Although Wilson is still active in the music industry, the early 1960s were his most fruitful years. He was able, in that dynamic, changing time, to convey to a receptive world the wonderful life of the surfers of the big California waves. Wilson's music has been an influence on other singer/songwriters such as Elton John, Billy Joel, Carly Simon, and Paul Simon.

TAMMY WYNETTE

Virginia Wynette Pugh (1942–1998) was born in Mississippi and worked on her family's cotton farm, picking cotton in the fields from the age of seven. In later years, she worked in a shoe factory, as a hairdresser, and as a beautician. Her singing career developed slowly at first and then in 1966, despite having no recording contract and a family to support, she made the fateful decision to move to Nashville. Her first single, "Apartment #9," exploded onto the country music charts, and her next eleven albums all hit number one. She became known as "The First Lady of Country Music," and her music traveled effortlessly around the world. One of her singles, "Stand by Your Man," is among the best-selling records of all time.

Many of her hits dealt with the traumas and losses in life: divorce, loneliness, and passion. Her emotional delivery and "tear in every note" style endeared her to her millions of fans around the world, and she went on to sell over 30 million albums and to gross more than $100 million.

Wynette suffered many years of serious health problems starting in the 1970s. She died in her sleep from a pulmonary blood clot, leaving a legacy of great music and an enduring influence on future country music performers.

Architects

Few things in modern life shout "America!" like the clean, uncluttered lines of a steel-and-glass skyscraper.

American architecture is the most visible manifestation of American life in cities around the world. The style of modern architecture in many countries today can be largely attributed to a few leading American architects of the late nineteenth and early twentieth centuries. Their influence is felt in the striking spareness of the style and their use of ever more modern materials. Where ancient Greek and Roman architecture uses columns and pediments, often as no more than symbols of power, with little value in terms of functionality, the unified theme of modern commercial buildings is nothing if not functionality. Where British Victorian commercial buildings were embossed with fancy scrollwork, magnificent shapely tiles, and tiny leaded-glass windows, modern buildings dispense with such frippery and pack in as much glass as a building can reasonably manage. Decoration, when used, is there mainly as a marketing tool.

Until the first reliable passenger elevator appeared in 1853, architects had been forever restricted in their imagination as to what could be built and used by pedestrians. There was very little appeal in building much above six stories. The occupants of the top floors were always compelled to use stairs, and, not unreasonably, top floors always attracted the lowest rent.

Three factors changed all that, and drove buildings to ever-greater heights. First, land prices within city boundaries began to sky rocket, which meant developers needed to maximize the use of the available space. Secondly, the development of high-tensile steel allowed architects to combine strength with lightness, when compared to building with stone masonry. Thirdly, the innovation that was Elisha Otis's elevator gave designers the opportunity to raise buildings to previously unfeasible heights. Once Otis had managed to prove the effectiveness of his safety features, an Otis elevator was installed into what is regarded as the world's first true skyscraper: the ten-story Home Insurance Building in Chicago. Once the commercial success of the first skyscraper had been seen, the landscape of cities around America began to change. The rest of the world was to follow over the next half century.

After the problem of getting people up and down very high buildings had been solved, the limits on height were blown away, and into this frenzy of opportunity stepped America's greatest architects.

WILLIAM Le BARON JENNEY (1832–1907)

Jenney, who was born in Massachusetts, is often referred to as the "father of the skyscraper," and was ranked number eighty-nine in *1,000 Years, 1,000 People,* a book of the world's 1,000 most influential people in the last millennium.

After a period constructing fortifications for Generals Sherman and Grant during the American Civil War, Jenney moved to Chicago in 1867 and became a leading light in the Chicago School of Architecture. He formed his own architectural practice, specializing in commercial buildings.

In 1885 it fell to Jenney to design the world's first steel-frame skyscraper, the Home Insurance Building in Chicago. The steel that Jenney used in its construction weighed only one third as much as a whole ten-story building using the more traditional materials of heavy masonry and concrete. This lighter construction also allowed much taller buildings to be constructed on the same area of land as would previously have been occupied by concrete and masonry buildings.

And another thing . . .

Jenney was a classmate and friend of Gustave Eiffel, the great French architect who went on to build the Eiffel Tower in Paris in 1890.

LOUIS SULLIVAN (1856–1924)

Sullivan has been called the "father of modernism" and the creator of the modern skyscraper. He strongly influenced Frank Lloyd Wright and inspired the work of the so-called Prairie School of architects. He was apprenticed to William Jenney for a time and was strongly influenced by his pioneering zeal.

Sullivan's great battle cry was "form follows function," and he maintained that aesthetics were of little use in commercial buildings. But in a classic display of "do as I say, not as I do," Sullivan himself did not dogmatically follow his own instructions. He allowed gross examples of Art Nouveau decoration to punctuate his structures, and for these he would use terra-cotta, cast iron, and other tactile materials.

Sullivan built the massive, golden-arched Transportation Building at the World's Colombian Exposition held in Chicago in 1893. Following well-publicized and heated disagreements with the director of the fair, Daniel Burnham, he claimed in his 1922 autobiography that the exposition had "set American architecture back half a century or more." Sullivan was surprised to find that his was the only building to receive extensive foreign recognition and that he had been awarded prestigious prizes for it.

Among the best of Sullivan's buildings are the Van Allen Building; the National Farmer's Bank in Owatonna; the Getty Tomb in Gracelands, Chicago; and the 1893 Chicago Stock Exchange Building.

Sadly, Louis Sullivan's career declined following the financial crash of 1893. His long-time business partner, who had been responsible for the marketing function in their partnership, left the business, and Sullivan failed to win major new commissions after the economy revived. He died alone and poor in a Chicago hotel room, a very sad end for a giant of his profession.

FRANK LLOYD WRIGHT (1867–1958)

It is no exaggeration to say that Frank Lloyd Wright was a disciple of Louis Sullivan. He was strongly influenced by Sullivan's teachings but went on to surpass his mentor in terms of influence and commercial success, and in the process became the most famous American architect of his age. In 1991 he was named the "greatest American architect of all time" by the American Institute of Architects. Wright designed more than 1,100 buildings, of which 500 were completed. Four hundred of these remain standing.

Wright was dismissed from Sullivan's practice after he was found accepting design commissions outside his employment. He went on in private practice to design many so-called Prairie Houses on the outskirts of Chicago and originated the open-plan design in domestic architecture, a style that is almost universally applied in modern houses. His designs were often characterized by long, flat exteriors.

Wright was always willing to experiment with uniquely shaped buildings. The Guggenheim Museum (1943–1949) in New York, which is built in the shape of a spiral (or helix), is an interesting example. He also introduced obtuse angles into his buildings, giving them a distinctive "Frank Lloyd Wright" appearance.

During his lifetime, Wright's private life attracted as much media coverage as his architecture. He changed his middle name from Lincoln to Lloyd to accentuate his Welsh ancestry, had seven children, and was married three times. He also ran off with a client's wife. While Wright was away on business, she was murdered along with six guests in his house.

Frank Lloyd Wright never attended architecture school.

> "A physician can bury his mistakes, but an architect can only advise his client to plant vines."
> **—Frank Lloyd Wright**

LUDWIG MIES van der ROHE (1886–1969)

He was born Maria Ludwig Michael Mies, in Aachen, Germany. With the rise of Nazism, Mies van der Rohe, as he became, emigrated to the United States in 1937, changing his name as he went. He added the "van der Rohe" to give himself a more distinguished air, and became an American citizen in 1944.

Although his early work was completed in Europe, with some memorable buildings such as the Tugendhat Villa in Brno, Czechoslovakia, it was in America that his influence was most keenly felt. He dismissed turn-of-the-century design, which imitated the Classical Era by using elaborate embellishment. Instead he thought on a grand scale and sought to define the twentieth century by the use of modern materials and uncluttered design. His use of industrial steel and plate glass to define exteriors set him apart from his contemporaries. He believed strongly in free-flowing internal space, which is now known as "open plan," and designed his buildings to be what he called "skin and bone."

He is known for his liberal use of the aphorisms "less is more" and "God is in the details" to express his design philosophy.

The Seagram Building in New York City stands today as a monument to Mies van der Rohe's talent. It is regarded as his most significant building, and during the erection phase, he introduced fast-track construction, in which design and construction take place concurrently.

Mies van der Rohe's architectural style was abstract, simple, and direct, and it has influenced a whole generation of today's practitioners.

"Architecture begins when one brick is placed carefully on top of another."

—Ludwig Mies van der Rohe

Writers

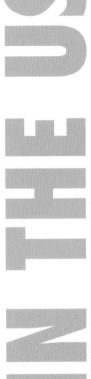

There is a long literary tradition in the USA, with its finest writers not only defining their own time, but also bringing the America of that era to the world. Here are some of the most influential.

EDGAR ALLAN POE (1809–1849)

Edgar Allan Poe is the acknowledged master of horror fiction, crime fiction, and detective fiction. He is generally recognized as having invented the detective story, creating the first fictional detective C. Auguste Dupin in 1871.

His works paved the way for future writers in the genre. Sir Arthur Conan Doyle, the creator of private detective Sherlock Holmes, said of Poe, "Each of Poe's detective stories is a root from which a whole literature has developed. Where was the detective story until Poe breathed life into it?"

Poe led an unconventional life. Having enlisted in the U.S. Army, he then deliberately arranged to be court-martialed to ensure dismissal. He left the army and married his thirteen-year-old cousin Virginia Clemm, in 1835. He met an unconventional death when he was found incoherent and in great distress on the streets of Baltimore. He was taken to the hospital but did not recover long enough to explain how he came to be in this condition. He died a few days later and the cause of his death remains a mystery. On the day of his burial, Poe's literary executor, Rufus Griswold, who was known to bear a grudge against him, published a long obituary under an assumed name. In it he said, "Edgar Allen Poe is dead . . . few will be grieved by it." Griswold tried to portray Poe as depraved and drug addled, although his claims were disproved later.

Poe's first book, an anthology of poetry, sold only fifty copies, but he went on to become one of the most influential of all American writers, with H. G. Wells, Fyodor Dostoevsky, and Jules Verne all acknowledging their debt to Poe's pioneering literature.

Poe's books remain in print, and still sell millions a year, almost two centuries after their first publication.

LOUISA MAY ALCOTT (1832–1888)

Louisa May Alcott served as a nurse in the American Civil War and in 1864 published her letters from this period in *Hospital Sketches*. In

1868, Alcott published *Little Women*, the novel that was to propel her to the pinnacle of literature. The book was a semiautobiographical account of her childhood and that of her sisters.

She wrote many other books, but none had the immediate impact and longevity of *Little Women*.

Alcott's work reflected women's issues in the so-called Gilded Age, when America's population and wealth exploded, and robber barons seemed set to rule the world.

MARK TWAIN (1835–1910)

Mark Twain, whose real name was Samuel Langhorne Clemens, worked first as a printer and later as a riverboat pilot. He tried his hand at gold mining and was also the editor of the *Territorial Enterprise*, a newspaper in Virginia City.

Famously, Clemens selected the pen name Mark Twain after the call from the sailors plumbing the river depths with rope and sinker. The rope would be marked at each fathom with a knot, and the depth called out to the boat's pilot. At two fathoms the sailor would call, "Mark twain."

Twain's first published book was *The Celebrated Jumping Frog of Calveras County* in 1865, and he published many others before creating his two greatest masterpieces, *The Adventures of Tom Sawyer* (1876) and *The Adventures of Huckleberry Finn* (1884). Both books drew heavily on his childhood experiences. *Tom Sawyer* tells the story of a mischievous orphan, who is adopted by his Aunt Polly, and who embarks on a series of adventures with his friends. His main adventures are getting lost in a cave, finding treasure, and playing pirates on the Mississippi. His girlfriend Becky Thatcher provides an innocent love interest. *Huckleberry Finn* is told in the first person and recounts the journey down the Mississippi of Finn and his friend, the escaped slave Jim. This book brings into focus the plight of slaves in the Deep South, and is a scathing attack on entrenched racist attitudes. This book is considered by many, with its descriptions of the drifting journey down the river, to be the most enduring image of escape and freedom in American literature.

Twain's most famous works provided vivid accounts of life on the Mississippi frontier to a nation hungry to learn more about its own history and to a world enchanted by Twain's rich language.

"Persons attempting to find a narrative in this story will be prosecuted; persons attempting to find a moral in it will be banished; persons attempting to find a plot in it will be shot."

—Mark Twain

(commenting on *The Adventures of Huckleberry Finn*)

DASHIELL HAMMETT (1894–1961)

Samuel Dashiell Hammett was born in Maryland, but also spent much of his young life in Philadelphia. He left school at fourteen to become a messenger boy at a local newspaper, where he progressed to newsboy, clerk, and timekeeper, and then left to try his hand at being a stevedore, loading and unloading ships, before leaving for New York. He joined the Pinkerton Detective Agency, in which he served as an operator on the "front line."

At this point it is worth saying a few words about the influence of the *Black Mask*, a "pulp" magazine launched in 1920 by H. L. Mencken and George Nathan. It started with the claim that it was "Five Magazines in One: the best stories of adventure, the best mystery and detective stories, the best love stories, the best romance stories and the best stories of the occult." The detective stories in the first few editions were disappointing, but in 1926 under new owners and a new editor, "Cap" Joseph Shaw, *Black Mask* began to publish the work of a new school of "hard-boiled" detective-story writers. Into this literary genre came Dashiell Hammett with his first story, "The Road Home."

Having established himself as a writer, Hammett published his first novel, *Red Harvest*, in 1929. Perhaps his best-known books are *The Thin Man* (1934) and *The Maltese Falcon* (1930), both of which were made into major Hollywood films.

Hammett's work was famed for being unsentimental and acutely observed and for reflecting American society of the 1920s and 1930s. Hammett is recognized as a pioneer in the field of the hard-boiled private detective novel.

Sadly, alcohol was to become an increasing blight on his life, and his later writing never matched the earlier output.

Hammett's writing influenced many writers, including the great Raymond Chandler.

And another thing . . .

In 1951, Hammett refused to reveal the names of his left-wing friends to the McCarthy-era House Un-American Activities Committee. Despite being a World War I veteran and having volunteered and served in the U.S. Army in World War II, he was sentenced to six months in jail.

RAYMOND CHANDLER (1888–1959)

Raymond Thornton Chandler was born in Chicago, but moved to Britain with his mother in 1895, after they were abandoned by his father. In 1907 Chandler became a naturalized British subject, and took a position at the British Admiralty, where he served for just over a year. He left to become a reporter on the *Daily Express* and soon thereafter published his first poem.

In 1917 Chandler enlisted in the Canadian Expeditionary Force and saw combat in the trenches in France. By the end of World War I he had joined the newly formed Royal Air Force and began to learn how to fly aircraft.

In 1919 Chandler returned to live in the United States and settled with his mother in Los Angeles, where he married. He worked his way up in the oil business and became a high-flying executive, but lost his job after prolonged bouts of alcoholism and absenteeism. In 1933 he began to write, like his predecessor Dashiell Hammett, for the *Black Mask* magazine. His first story was "Blackmailers Don't Shoot," which was published in 1933.

Chandler's writing evokes the tough life on the streets and in the underworld of Los Angeles of the 1940s and 1950s. The first of his great novels, *The Big Sleep*, was published in 1939. His other major works include *Farewell My Lovely*, *The High Window*, and *The Long Goodbye*.

SINCLAIR LEWIS (1885–1951)

In 1930, Sinclair Lewis secured his place in the history of American literature when he became the first American to win the Nobel Prize for Literature.

His work is known for its critical view of capitalism and American society, and particularly his powerful characterization of women. He was first published in 1912 and had completed a few novels and a succession

WRITERS

153

of "potboilers" by 1920. It was at this time that he decided to devote himself full-time to serious writing. In October 1920 he published *Main Street*, which took the publishing world by storm; it is estimated that Lewis became a millionaire simply from the royalties. Later works include *Elmer Gantry* and *Babbitt*, for which he refused the Pulitzer Prize.

Lewis suffered from alcoholism for much of his working life and it finally overtook him in Rome.

> "In other countries art and literature are left to a lot of bums living in attics and feeding on booze and spaghetti, but in America the successful writer or picture painter is indistinguishable from any other decent business man."
>
> **—Sinclair Lewis**

EUGENE O'NEILL (1888–1953)

Eugene O'Neill's plays were among the first to introduce realism into American drama. His work followed in the tradition of Anton Chekhov and Henrik Ibsen, and his plays are still performed around the world today.

The characters he created are generally on the fringes of society and engage in depraved behavior. The speeches were the first written in American vernacular.

O'Neill was awarded the Pulitzer Prize for Drama three times, and in 1936 he won the Nobel Prize for Literature. He suffered from depression and alcoholism and died in the Sheraton Hotel in Boston. His last words are reputed to have been, "Born in a hotel room, and Goddammit, died in one."

His autobiographical masterpiece, *Long Day's Journey into Night*, was published posthumously in 1956.

And another thing . . .

At eighteen, O'Neill's daughter Oona married Charlie Chaplin, who was fifty-four. O'Neill never spoke to her again.

F. SCOTT FITZGERALD (1896–1940)

Francis Scott Key Fitzgerald was born in St. Paul, Minnesota.

His masterpiece, *The Great Gatsby*, was published in 1925. It captured the spirit of the Jazz Age—that period in American history when it seemed to the rest of the world that, in America, if you tried hard enough, you could achieve anything.

The book revealed Fitzgerald's fascination with the very rich and their behavior. He drew inspiration from his wife Zelda's tempestuous personality and used their marriage as the basis for some of his stories. It was to prove a mixed blessing. Believing he had used some of the contents of her diaries in his writing, she said in an interview after the breakdown of their marriage, "In fact, Mr. Fitzgerald—I believe that is how he spells his name—seems to believe plagiarism begins at home."

A lifetime of alcoholism damaged Fitzgerald's health, and he died prematurely after a heart attack at the home of a friend.

Fitzgerald's writing influenced the work of Ernest Hemingway, who said of him, "His talent was as natural as the pattern that was made by the dust on a butterfly's wing."

Fitzgerald's elegant and pure prose ensured that his would be the voice of the American Jazz Age that was heard around the world.

> "Let me tell you about the very rich. They are different from you and me." (*The Great Gatsby*)
> **—F. Scott Fitzgerald**

WILLIAM FAULKNER (1897–1962)

William Faulkner is one of the most influential writers of the twentieth century, and is among the most highly regarded American novelists of all time. He was awarded the Nobel Prize for Literature in 1949. His Nobel citation read, "for his powerful and artistically unique contribution to the modern American novel." Faulkner used half of the prize money to set up a fund to "support and encourage new writers."

A Mississippi resident for most of his life, he was considered one of the most important Southern writers, alongside Mark Twain and Tennessee Williams. His characters are often Southerners, and he features the tragic plight of blacks in this society.

Faulkner also tried his hand at screenwriting in Hollywood, working there with Humphrey Bogart and Lauren Bacall at the invitation of the great director Howard Hawks. He was also a pioneer of the stream-of-consciousness style of writing, which has influenced many other writers around the world.

And another thing . . .

The original spelling of Faulkner's surname was "Falkner." It has never been established how this minor change came about, although it was rumored to be a simple copywriting error.

MARGARET MITCHELL (1900–1949)

Margaret Mitchell was born in Atlanta, Georgia, and moved to Northampton, Massachusetts, to study for a medical degree. She turned instead to journalism. After marrying in 1925 she embarked on her only novel: *Gone with the Wind*. It took ten years and was published in 1936.

The novel was set in the Old South in the time of the American Civil War and chronicled the immense changes in Southern society during that period. The book, which ran to more than one thousand pages (or 460,000 words), won the Pulitzer Prize for the Novel in 1937. It was translated into thirty languages and made into the most widely viewed film in history. The book broke all publication records: it sold 50,000 copies in one day, 1 million in six months, and 2 million in twelve months. By 1976, worldwide sales had reached over 20 million, and it continues to sell today.

Although this was her only novel, Margaret Mitchell stands as the popular chronicler of that dramatic era in American history, and despite her enormous success, she remained modest all her life. In 1949, on the way to the theater, she walked into the path of an oncoming car and was killed instantly.

"After all, tomorrow is another day."

—Margaret Mitchell

(final line from Gone with the Wind)

JOHN STEINBECK (1902–1968)

John Ernest Steinbeck III was born and brought up in Salinas, California, and trained to become a marine biologist. To fund his writing, he took on work as an agricultural laborer and a semiskilled technician.

In 1935 he published *Tortilla Flat*, which told the story of the changing "paisanos" of California, foreshadowing his later work. 1937 saw the publication of *Of Mice and Men*, which tells the story of two displaced migrant workers in California during the Great Depression.

The Grapes of Wrath—his major work published in 1939—characterized the terrible fate of the poor in the face of the disaster of failed harvests. The book was set in the time of the Great Depression of the 1930s, in the 100 million acres around Oklahoma that became known as the Dust Bowl. The story, which drew on Steinbeck's own experiences as a reporter, follows a family in their quest to find a better life in the West. Steinbeck won the 1940 Pulitzer Prize for Fiction with this book and was awarded the 1962 Nobel Prize for Literature.

After his death, the *New York Times* said: "His place in US literature is secure. It lives on in the works of innumerable writers who learned from him how to present the forgotten man unforgettably."

"The free exploring mind of the individual human is the most valuable thing in the world."
—John Steinbeck's epitaph,
which he wrote himself

ERNEST HEMINGWAY (1899–1961)

Ernest Millar Hemingway was born into a comfortable middle-class family in Chicago. His parents wanted him to study to become a professional violinist, but he preferred the cut and thrust of journalism and joined the *Kansas City Star* as a "cub" reporter. While he was employed at the newspaper, he spent a great deal of time studying their style book and developed the use of short, declarative sentences, in which the speaker makes a positive statement, such as "I am going fishing." Hemingway made a great deal of his reputation with this sort of punchy writing.

He saw service in World War I as an ambulance driver. His work brought him close to the fighting, and he was badly wounded on the Italian front. After returning to the United States, he wrote newspaper articles and married for the first time. In 1921 Hemingway returned to Europe, and settled into the life of a roving correspondent. It was during this period of his life that he spent time with F. Scott Fitzgerald, Gertrude Stein, Ezra Pound, and James Joyce, and in 1923 he published *Three Stories and Ten Poems*. The book had only limited circulation, but he went on to publish *In Our Time* (1924), *The Sun Also Rises* (1926), and *Men without Women* (1927). The writings of the young Hemingway are thought by many critics to be the truest voice of the Lost Generation—that group of restless, searching young Americans who lived and roamed the world after World War I.

He employed a distinctive style that was economical with words and understated in descriptive passages. In *The Old Man and the Sea*, Hemingway writes of the main character, Santiago, a fisherman: "Santiago picked the mast up and put it on his shoulder and started up the road. He sat down five times before he reached his shack." His writing was strongly influenced by that of the great short-story writer Ring Lardner.

Hemingway's body of work, which also included *A Farewell to Arms*, *Death in the Afternoon*, *Green Hills in Africa*, and *For Whom the Bell Tolls*, resulted in his being awarded the 1954 Nobel Prize in Literature.

Hemingway said of himself, "I had learned already never to empty the well of my writing, but always to stop when there was still something there in the deep part of the well and let it refill at night from the springs that fed it."

At the age of sixty-two, he took his own life with a shotgun.

HARPER LEE (b. 1926)

Nelle Harper Lee, like Margaret Mitchell, only wrote one novel— but what a novel.

To Kill a Mockingbird was published in 1960 and won the Pulitzer Prize for Fiction in 1961. With refreshing modesty, Lee said in 1964: "I never expected any sort of success with *Mockingbird*. I was hoping for a quick and merciful death at the hands of the reviewers, but at the same time I sort of hoped someone would like it enough to give me encouragement. Public encouragement. I hoped for a little, as I said, but I got rather a whole lot and in some ways this was just about as frightening as the quick merciful death I'd expected."

In this, her seminal novel, the theme is racial injustice in the Deep South. The story focuses specifically on the injustice dealt out to a black man who is wrongly accused of a crime. The whole book is seen through the eyes of a young white girl and depicts the characters in a small Southern town. The mockingbird of the title is the literary representation of the victim of the injustice, the innocent black farm laborer. *To Kill a Mockingbird* is widely used as a set text in schools all over the world, and has sold over 30 million copies worldwide. In 1999 it was voted the "Best Novel of the Century" by *Library Journal*. In 2007, U.S. president George W. Bush presented Harper Lee with the Presidential Medal of Freedom, and in his speech he described Lee's great book as "a gift to the world."

Since publication of *To Kill a Mockingbird*, Lee has written no more books for publication, although she came close to finishing a work of nonfiction, which she set aside.

Lee was born in Monroeville, Alabama and grew up with Truman Capote as a childhood friend. She was also a descendant of Robert E. Lee (1807–1870), the Civil War Commander, who was himself descended from King Robert II of Scotland.

> "Shoot all the bluejays you want, if you can hit 'em, but remember it's a sin to kill a mockingbird."
> (*To Kill a Mockingbird*)
>
> **—Harper Lee**

JACK KEROUAC (1922–1969)

John Louis (Jack) Kerouac is the best known of the Beat Generation writers.

His writing has influenced a diverse range of other writers and performers including Hunter S. Thomson, Haruki Murakami, Bob Dylan, Jim Morrison, and Simon and Garfunkel. Kerouac himself was influenced by jazz and Buddhism.

Kerouac was born in Lowell, Massachusetts, part Native American through his mother's family. He didn't learn to speak English until he was six years old, as his family spoke only French. After school and several dead-end jobs, including a spell on the construction gang that built the Pentagon, he joined the U.S. Navy. He was discharged after one month. On his discharge papers it was stated that he was of "indifferent character."

His novel *On the Road* set the American experience apart from those of other countries. The sheer distances from town to town, the freedom to travel, the different ways of diverse peoples, the easy friendships, the exotic and the indifferent food, the music that touched the soul of the narrator; all served to show the possibilities held out by life in the United States. Kerouac's writing chronicled the Beat Generation's desperate search for identity and purpose.

On the Road, which took Kerouac more than seven years to write, was published in 1957. It is the iconic novel of that period of American history, but remains in print around the world today.

> "In actuality there was only a handful of real hip swinging cats and what there was vanished mightily swiftly during the Korean War when a sinister new kind of efficiency appeared in America—the generation itself was shortlived and small in number."
>
> **—Jack Kerouac,**
> commenting on the Beat Generation

Kerouac had an unusual method of writing. He taped together sheets of tracing paper until he had a roll around 120 feet long. Then he fed it into his typewriter and typed continuously until the roll was finished. This method, which allowed him to type without having to change paper, helped Kerouac to "flow" without interruption.

JOSEPH HELLER (1923–1999)

Joseph Heller was born in Coney Island, New York, and became one of the great satirical voices of the post–World War II period.

In his youth, he held several jobs, including a year as a blacksmith's apprentice. After service in the U.S. Army Air Corps in World War II, during which he flew on sixty missions as a bombardier, Heller studied English, taught composition, and worked as a copywriter at an advertising agency.

In 1953, Heller came up with the idea for a novel, with the working title of *Catch-18*. A publisher agreed to take the book, which had been only partially completed, paid an advance of $750 and promised another $750 for the completed manuscript. Heller missed his deadline by nearly five years.

The title of the book was changed to *Catch-22* shortly before its publishing date to avoid confusion with *Leon Uris's* new novel *Mila-18*.

The book was a satire on the futility of war and the title has become the by-word (in much of the world) for situations in which the protagonist is trapped by rules and bureaucracy. A Catch-22 situation is one in which all apparent options are futile as perverse logic means that only one outcome is possible.

> "Frankly I'd like to see the government get out of war altogether and leave the whole field to private industry."
>
> **—Joseph Heller**

TOM WOLFE (b. 1931)

Thomas Kennerly Wolfe, Jr. was born in Richmond, Virginia. After turning down Princeton, he received a doctorate in American studies from Yale University. Wolfe went on to become the leading proponent of the literary style known as New Journalism, for which the guidelines are:

- Tell the story using scenes rather than historical narrative.
- Recreate dialogue in full.
- Use a first-person point of view.
- Record everyday details such as behavior, possessions, friends, and family.

New Journalism used onomatopoeia and multiple exclamation points to emphasize the point being made.

Hunter S. Thompson, Truman Capote, P. J. O'Rourke, and Norman Mailer all demonstrate techniques of New Journalism in their writing.

Wolfe's major novel was *Bonfire of the Vanities* (1987), which portrayed life in New York during the 1980s, when bankers and dealers had become the so-called Masters of the Universe.

And another thing . . .

Wolfe has worn his trademark white suit since 1962. He bought the first white suit to wear in the summer but found it too heavy. He wore it as a winter suit and found it created something of a sensation, so he decided to keep it as part of his persona.

GORE VIDAL (b. 1925)

Eugene Luther Vidal Jr. was born to a military/political family within the military academy at West Point, New York.

He began writing during military service and in 1948 his novel *The City and the Pillar* became the first major American novel to feature unambiguous homosexuality. A prolific playwright, novelist, and non-fiction writer, he is regarded as a bellwether of American society and one of the premier humorists of the age. His work has been sold around the world and according to his biographer, Fred Kaplan, "No other twentieth century figure has moved so easily and confidently, and had such a profound effect, in the disparate worlds of literature, drama, film, politics, historical debate, and the culture wars."

"Whenever a friend succeeds, a little something in me dies."

—Gore Vidal

MARIO PUZO (1920–1999)

Mario Puzo was born in the Hell's Kitchen neighborhood of Manhattan and lived with his six brothers and sisters above the railway yards.

He attended Columbia University and then worked in various jobs including government office work and freelance journalism.

Puzo wrote two novels, *Dark Arena* and *Fortunate Pilgrim*, before his most famous work, *The Godfather*, which was published in 1969. *The Godfather* changed the public's perception of life within the Mafia, as it explored the themes of love, family loyalties, and Old World values. The story is set within the context of a highly influential criminal organization.

The Godfather remained on the *New York Times* bestseller list for many months, and Puzo's is undeniably an authentic American literary voice, but the book is not quite regarded as great literature. It did, however, have an enormous impact on American and European culture. The phrase, "I'll make him an offer he can't refuse," which means "accept my terms or pay a very high price—perhaps your life," derived from the book and has passed into common usage.

The main character, Don Corleone, was portrayed as having great skill in building up banks of high-level friends. He accomplished this by offering favors and services, which he "banked" for future calling in. But Puzo also managed to make him into an admirable, even likeable figure. Many of the values expressed in the book highlight the decline in the same values outside the family. Although it is a work of fiction, *The Godfather* seemed to reveal a great deal about the influence of powerful crime syndicates in general society.

"A lawyer with a briefcase can steal more than a hundred men with guns." (*The Godfather*)

—Mario Puzo

ERICA JONG (b. 1942)

Erica Jong was born in New York City and is best known for her first novel, *Fear of Flying*, which was published in 1973. This book has now sold over 18 million copies worldwide.

Fear of Flying is written in the first person and explores women's sexual desires. It was published at a time when women were taking major steps to full emancipation. The heroine uses sex as a means both of personal pleasure and a way to achieve happiness. She does not, as with most sexually free women in fiction, come to a disastrous end. Jong's book was especially influential with the generation of women who were young at the time of its publication.

> "Every country gets the circus it deserves. Spain gets bullfights. Italy gets the Catholic Church. America gets Hollywood."
>
> **—Erica Jong**

TONI MORRISON (b. 1931)

Toni Morrison was awarded the Nobel Prize for Literature in 1993, the first black woman to be so honored. Her Nobel citation read: "Toni Morrison, who in novels characterized by visionary force and poetic import, gives life to an essential aspect of American reality."

Morrison's novel *Beloved* won the 1988 Pulitzer Prize for Literature. The book is partly based on the real life of a slave, Margaret Garner, and confronts several of the most grotesque aspects of slavery, such as sexual abuse and violence. Morrison's intention was to make the reader become active in the story and to work out what is actually going on plotwise.

As a child in Lorain, Ohio, she read many of the classics of literature, including works by Leo Tolstoy and Jane Austen, and in 1949 she entered Howard University to study English. She later went to Cornell.

Following the breakdown of her marriage, Morrison moved to New York. Once there, she worked for some years as an editor at Random House and was instrumental in bringing African American literature into the mainstream.

> "You need intelligence and you need to look. You need a gaze, a wide gaze, penetrating and roving—that's what's useful for art."
>
> **—Toni Morrison,**
> speaking during an interview on the *Oprah Winfrey Show* about what she believes constitutes the essential requirements of a writer

Fashion Designers

During the last quarter of the twentieth century, American fashion houses made major inroads into the public fashion market. Previously they were better known for the more specialized area of movie-industry clothing.

America's main competitors, the French, Italian, and British fashion houses, often display outrageous designs that are unwearable in public. The most successful of the American fashion houses offer glamour and high fashion that is wearable straight from the shop.

BILL BLASS (1922–2002)

In 1946, after serving in the U.S. Army during World War II, Bill Blass left his hometown of Fort Wayne, Indiana, for New York. After twenty years of success designing for others, he established his own fashion house in 1970 by buying the old established firm of Maurice Rentner Limited and renaming it Bill Blass Limited. He planned to work full time in the fashion industry, and became known for his sporty but sophisticated women's wear. His designs combined clean lines and high-class glamour, and his clothes have met with success throughout Europe and Asia as well as America.

Among his clients were three of America's First Ladies, Jackie Kennedy, Nancy Reagan, and Barbara Bush, and by 1998, sales had grown to $700 million.

The *New York Times* said of Blass, "He took American sportswear to its highest level."

TOM FORD (b. 1961)

Tom Ford made his name in the world of international fashion by turning around the declining fortunes of the Italian fashion house Gucci. He joined Gucci in 1990, and when they acquired the Yves Saint Laurent (YSL) brand in 1994, he was appointed creative director of both brands.

Although the main shareholder, Maurizio Gucci, always wanted Gucci designs to be "round and brown," Ford continued with his own ideas, which were "square and black." Ford also adopted an innovative marketing approach, using top photographer Mario Testino (b. 1954), to produce award-winning images of Gucci products. His new approach catapulted the brands back to their position at the top of the fashion world. When Ford joined Gucci, it was close to bankruptcy but by the time he left in 2004 it was valued at $4.3 billion.

After Ford parted company with Gucci in 2004, he set up his own fashion house, Tom Ford, and now has boutiques in New York, Zurich, and Toronto.

EDITH HEAD (1897–1981)

Edith Claire Head won eight Oscars, more than any other woman in any category. Her designs were known for their elegant restraint, and were influential around the world.

By the 1930s, Head had established herself as Hollywood's leading costume designer, working first at Paramount and later at Universal Pictures. Her clothing was in dozens of films, and she worked extensively with the leading directors of the day, including Alfred Hitchcock, Hal Wallis, and George Roy Hill.

The list of stars she clothed reads like a lineup of Hollywood "royalty." They include Ginger Rogers, Bette Davis, Barbara Stanwyck, Shirley MacLaine, Ingrid Bergman, Mae West, Dorothy Lamour, Hedy Lamarr, Gloria Swanson, Elizabeth Taylor, Grace Kelly, Marlene Dietrich, Rita Hayworth, Kim Novak, Audrey Hepburn, and Sophia Loren.

TOMMY HILFIGER (b. 1951)

In his late teens, Thomas Jacob Hilfiger opened his first business, a boutique called The People's Place in Elmira, New York. By the time he was twenty-five, Hilfiger's shop had gone bust, so he turned his attention away from the retailing end of the fashion business and tried to break into the design side of clothing.

In the early 1980s, he turned down an offer to join Calvin Klein as a designer. In 1984 he founded Tommy Hilfiger Corporation and began to build his brand. The Hilfiger style is easily recognizable, featuring highly distinctive design features like stripes and primary colors. By 2004, annual revenues had reached $1.8 billion worldwide, and he was employing more than 5,000 people.

Hilfiger sold the business in 2006 for $1.6 billion.

And another thing . . .

In May 2006 Hilfiger picked a fight with Guns N' Roses frontman Axl Rose at Rosario Dawson's birthday party. He had to be led away (kicking and screaming) by his own security guards. Fortunately for Hilfiger, Rose displayed admirable self-restraint, and did not throw any punches.

MARC JACOBS (b. 1963)

Marc Jacobs is the head designer of his own clothing line, and also creative director of the French design house, Louis Vuitton.

In 1987, Jacobs became the youngest ever winner of the Perry Award for New Fashion Talent, presented annually by the Council of Fashion Designers of America. The Perry Award is the fashion industry equivalent of an Oscar. After winning the Perry Award, Jacobs's designs were seen in all the major fashion shows, and he became a major influence on younger fashion designers. His designs often hark back to an earlier age, and some rivals claim he is therefore merely a copyist.

As well as outlets throughout America, Jacobs has shops in London, Paris, Madrid, Copenhagen, and Moscow.

DONNA KARAN (b. 1948)

Donna Karan began selling clothing in New York at age fourteen. In 1968, after two years at the Parsons New School for Design, she took up a position at Anne Klein. Klein died in 1974 but Karan carried on as head designer and remained there until 1989. She left Klein to set up her own label, and launched her now world famous brand DKNY (Donna Karan New York) in 1990.

By 1997 most of the DKNY merchandise had become a world brand, and was being licensed to other retailers to market (Liz Claiborne for jeans, Estée Lauder for cosmetics, Phillips–Van Heusen for shirts). DKNY also owns their own stores in London, Hong Kong, Dubai, Tel Aviv, Tokyo, Antwerp, and many other cities.

In 2001 the immense French luxury goods group LVMH acquired the DKNY brand for $243 million.

CALVIN KLEIN (b. 1942)

Calvin Klein founded his eponymous business in 1968 with $10,000. His first venture was a coat shop in the York Hotel in New York, and he began to design and produce his trademark sleek and elegant clothing range a year later. In Vogue magazine, Klein was soon described as "the supreme master of minimalism."

In 1985, Calvin Klein merchandise was bringing in over $600 million in worldwide sales revenue, and the range was being sold in over 12,000 shops around the world. However, by 1992 things had taken a dramatic turn for the worse, and the company faced insolvency. Klein himself retook the reins and managed to ramp up the profits through the 1990s. The CK range of men's underwear was visible on billboards in New York, London, Milan, Paris, and Tokyo. Klein's masterstroke was to display the male underwear on female models.

In 1993, the Council of Fashion Designers of America named Calvin Klein America's Best Designer. In 2002, Philips Van Heusen acquired the company, and Klein stayed on as creative head of collections.

RALPH LAUREN (b. 1939)

Ralph Lauren (born Ralph Lifshitz) is known throughout the world for his distinctive Polo range of clothing and fragrances.

After serving in the U.S. Army from 1962 to 1964, Lauren held down a sales job in Brooks Brothers in New York before starting a necktie shop in 1967. The shop provided an outlet for selling ties of his own design, and exclusively used the Polo brand name for the first time.

In 1970 he launched a range of women's suits using classic men's tailoring and used the Polo emblem of a polo player on horseback.

Lauren's designs are known for their portrayal of Old World charm and opulence and have been the inspiration for designers throughout the world. Lauren himself has film star looks and is the "poster boy" for his own designs.

The Ralph Lauren group is conservatively estimated to be worth in excess of $1 billion.

Unlikely

Inventors

Other nationalities, looking from the outside, believe American culture has no fear of failure—no embarrassment in having tried but not quite made it. Some countries are ruled by rigid hierarchical systems that stifle any creativity before it's had the chance to develop. Citizens of totalitarian states have few opportunities to try anything. Lives are restricted to doing little more than obeying the orders of the controlling state government apparatus.

This is not the case in the USA, where the freedom to think is embedded in the culture. Outsiders can see that the American "system" fosters an atmosphere of creative endeavor, which in turn encourages men and women to willingly try their hands at inventing. Being famous in one field is no barrier to inventing something to improve another.

Benjamin Franklin (1706–1790) is an early example of someone skilled in one field (diplomacy and statesmanship) who used his keen powers of observation and imagination to invent many products. He developed the first bifocal lenses for spectacles, the lightning conductor, the armonica (a musical instrument that uses drinking glasses to create notes), and the carriage odometer (mileometer). The product for which he is best remembered is the Franklin stove, which improved on the performance of open fireplaces. The stove used special baffles at the rear to direct the air current and reduce smoke. At the same time the stove provides more heat. Franklin never applied for a patent, stating that he was grateful for all the products he could use for free, and wished others to benefit from his inventions.

PRESIDENT INVENTORS

GEORGE WASHINGTON (1732–1799)

For the first part of his life, Washington was a very successful farmer, having grown up on a farm in Virginia. By his early teenage years he had mastered tobacco growing and the raising of stock. In 1752, up on the death of his brother, he inherited the 2,500-acre Mount Vernon Estate, and went on to increase the landholding to around 8,000 acres.

> "Government is not reason, it is not eloquence, it is force; like fire, a troublesome servant and a fearful master. Never for a moment should it be left to irresponsible action."
> **—George Washington**

The Seeding Plow

The seeding plow, which combines the two operations of plowing the land and distributing seed, has been around in crude form since the Mesopotamian civilization between 5000 and 4000 BCE. In all that time, it had hardly been improved.

Washington, who was supreme in his knowledge of farming, applied his creative talent. By redesigning the seeding plow so that seeds were distributed at an even rate, rather than scattered randomly, he made the plow 60 percent more effective, and in the belief that his new design would enhance the lives of the common man, he deliberately did not register it as a patent.

Wine Coaster

Another invention by George Washington, of which we know little, is the wine coaster. It is believed he invented the coaster to prevent the pristine linen tablecloths at the White House from being marked by circles of red wine from the bottom of glasses. As with the seeding plow, Washington did not make a patent application.

THOMAS JEFFERSON (1743–1826)

> "I hope we shall crush in its birth, the aristocracy of our moneyed corporations which dare already to challenge our government to a trial of strength."
> **—Thomas Jefferson**

Thomas Jefferson was one of the founders of the United States of America and served as its third president from 1801 to 1809. He is well known as one of the principal authors of the Declaration of

Independence (1776). The major event during his presidency was the Louisiana Purchase, which effectively doubled the size of the United States, and today accounts for around 23 percent of U.S. land. However, Jefferson was not only a great political figure but also had a highly inventive turn of mind . . .

Swivel Chair

In 1768, work began on Monticello, the house that now sits on Jefferson's 552-acre estate. Although he moved into Monticello during 1770, work was not completed on the building until the end of his presidency in 1809. Jefferson was an accomplished architect and designer, and introduced into the new house his own invention of a swivel chair, the first of its type known.

The basic design is now used in modern swivel chairs, but Jefferson did not file a patent.

Macaroni Machine

During his time serving as ambassador to France, Jefferson acquired a taste for French and Italian cooking, and on his return, he brought a French cook to the United States. He designed an improved macaroni machine through which dough was extruded to create the macaroni shape.

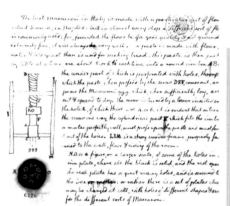

Wheel Cipher

Jefferson served as George Washington's secretary of state from 1790 to 1793. During the period of this appointment, European postmasters were suspected of opening and reading all correspondence. To counter this intrusion into State secrets, Jefferson devised a twenty-six-piece wooden wheel cipher to provide a secure method of encoding and decoding messages. Although the codes were thought at the time to be unbreakable, the wheel cipher was abandoned in 1802.

> "I think this is the most extraordinary collection of talent that has ever been gathered together at the White House—with the possible exception of when Thomas Jefferson dined alone."
>
> **—U.S. President John F. Kennedy,**
> in welcoming forty-nine Nobel Prize winners to the White House in 1962

ABRAHAM LINCOLN (1809–1865)

> "I am a slow walker, but I never walk back."
>
> **—Abraham Lincoln**

Abraham Lincoln was the sixteenth president of the United States. An outspoken opponent of the expansion of slavery, he led the country through the greatest turmoil in its history, the American Civil War. At the dedication of the Soldiers National Cemetery in Gettysburg, Lincoln gave one of the great speeches of history, now known as The Gettysburg Address. He described the ceremony as an opportunity to honor the dead and consecrate the living, so that "government of the people, by the people, for the people, shall not perish from the earth." As the conflict drew to a close, Lincoln was assassinated at the theater by John Wilkes Booth.

Lincoln had tried more than one career. At one time, he had been a mill manager, then a postmaster, and a lawyer, before turning to politics. He also had an inventive turn of mind.

Bouyancy Chamber

During his travels throughout America, many of which involved river journeys, Lincoln had noticed that the shallow-draft riverboats became unstable in shallow waters and had an alarming tendency to tip. He set about designing a device to give the boats added stability. In 1849, he received U.S. Patent #6,469 for an air-filled buoyancy chamber, which is now called a sponson. The idea behind the device was to provide additional buoyancy when fitted to the sides of shallow-draft vessels in the shallow waters of some rivers.

The invention did not enjoy commercial success, but it is unique in the annals of the United States Patent and Trademark Office, being the only patent ever to be held by an inventor who would go on to become president of the USA.

FILM STARS, ENTERTAINERS, AND SPORTSMEN AS INVENTORS

HEDY LAMARR (1914–2000)

Hedy Lamarr (see also "torpedoes" and "cell phones") was one of the great Hollywood beauties of the 1930s and 1940s, appearing in such box-office hits as *The Ziegfeld Follies*. She achieved notoriety in 1933 when she appeared in the film *Ecstasy*, and entered the history books as the first woman to appear on screen clearly having an orgasm. The film was produced in Czechoslovakia, and was the first to be blocked by U.S. Customs, under the Indecency Acts, from entering the USA.

Packet Switching

Lamarr has been inducted into the Inventors Hall of Fame as the inventor of a system of radio-frequency switching known as packet switching. The system, which allows frequencies to be switched very rapidly, was first developed and patented by Lamarr in 1941 for torpedo guidance systems. At the time of World War I, if enemy ships were able to block its radio guidance signal, a torpedo had the alarming tendency, if it missed its primary target, of circling round and coming back to sink the ship that fired it. Using packet switching, the signal to the torpedo could be maintained until it hit the enemy ship.

Packet switching is now used in the cell phone industry to enable callers to move from area to area (frequency cell to frequency cell) without losing the signal.

Lamarr allowed her patent, which was one of the most important of all time, to lapse, thus missing out on one of the greatest financial bonanzas in history.

STEVE McQUEEN (1930–1980)

McQueen was a skilled race car driver. Learning from the experience of sitting behind the wheels of powerful cars for long periods of time, he came to understand what was needed to maintain the body position of the car driver and to help prevent fatigue. He invented the bucket seat. The idea of the bucket seat is to hold the body in a comfortable position and prevent unwanted sideways rocking.

MARLON BRANDO (1924–2004)

In 2001, Brando patented a drumhead-tensioning device.

By connecting a drumhead via cables to a tuning ring, tension on the drumhead can be adjusted by rotating the link.

DANNY KAYE (1913–1987)

Kaye invented and patented a children's blowout toy similar to those that unravel when blown. The main distinguishing feature of Kaye's invention is the large number of parts that unravel at the same time.

ZEPPO MARX (1901–1979)

Zeppo Marx (real name Herbert Manfred Marx), developed a stage and screen persona as an amiable straight man in contrast to his madcap brothers. However, away from the show-business spotlight Zeppo was a serious inventor.

After a friend suffered a heart attack in the middle of a golf course, he began work on a cardiac heart pulse-rate monitor, and in 1969 he was issued patent #3,473,526. The device was worn on the wrist and monitored the wearer's heart. It sounded an alarm if he or she went into cardiac arrest.

Unknown to the fans of his show-business act, Marx was a skilled engineering designer and the owner of an engineering company called Marman Products. He invented the heavy-duty Marman Clamp, which secured the atomic bomb within the *Enola Gay*, the aircraft that flew to Hiroshima.

MARK TWAIN (1835–1910)

> "Noise proves nothing. Often a hen that has merely laid an egg cackles as if she had laid an asteroid."
> **—Mark Twain**

Twain (real name: Samuel Langhorne Clemens) wrote some of the most memorable literature ever written by an American. For the three years up to the outbreak of the American Civil War in 1861, Twain served as a riverboat pilot on the Mississippi.

His remarkably creative mind also turned to inventions. These included a bed clamp for infants (to prevent them from falling out of bed), a revolutionary type of steam engine, photographic processing, and a form of typesetting machine that was so fast that it astounded the people who witnessed the demonstration. Unfortunately for Twain, the typesetting machine proved to be unreliable as a result of manufacturing faults, and it was superseded by the Linotype machine before he was able to bring it to commercial success.

JAMIE LEE CURTIS (b. 1958)

Jamie Lee Curtis, the daughter of Tony Curtis and Janet Leigh and a Hollywood star herself, invented a multipiece infant garment that includes a modified diaper. Her garment has an openable, moisture-proof pocket containing wipes that can be taken out with one hand. She filed the patent in 1987, but will not allow it to be brought to market until diapers are biodegradable.

Curtis is married to the 5th Baron Haden-Guest and is formally titled Lady Haden-Guest. Before he inherited the title from his father in 1996, her husband was known as Christopher Guest, a writer, comic actor, musician, and director.

HARRY HOUDINI (1874–1926)

Houdini (real name Ehrich Weiss) invented and patented a deep-sea-diving suit.

MICHAEL JACKSON (b. 1958)

Jackson invented a device to give the impression of defying gravity. The idea is for a person to lean forward beyond their center of gravity, and yet remain standing.

The contraption includes a shoe with a specially designed slot within the heel. The shoe engages with a hitch member (a form of hook) set into the stage surface so that the wearer can slide the shoe into the locked position and lean forward without falling over. When that part of the act is complete, the performer can slide the shoe away from the hitch member without the audience being able to see how it works.

GARY BURGHOFF (b.1943)

Burghoff, who played Radar O'Reilly in *M*A*S*H*, is the inventor of the Chum Magic fishing lure, which attracts fish toward a boat.

JULIE NEWMAR (b. 1933)

Julie Newmar was one of the most beautiful Hollywood actresses of the 1950s and 1960s. She invented a panty girdle with a shaping band to enhance the derriere. She also founded a business to market the products.

TOM LEHRER (b.1928)

"I went from adolescence to senility, trying to bypass maturity."

—Tom Lehrer

Lehrer invented the Jell-O shot, a Jell-O cube made with half water and half hard liquor.

PAUL WINCHELL (1922–2005)

Winchell's career as one of America's top ventriloquists spanned almost sixty years. As a skilled voice artist, he was the voice of Tigger in the Disney adaptation of A. A. Milne's *Winnie The Pooh*, and the voice of Dick Dastardly in the Hanna-Barbera cartoons. Aside from his career as a ventriloquist, Winchell was also a professional hypnotist, an acupuncturist, and the writer of many articles on theology.

He kept busy by registering thirty patents, including one for a frozen-food indicator, which showed when food had deteriorated after a power cut. He registered another for a type of disposable razor.

Winchell's most important invention was an early design for an artificial heart, which he donated free of charge to the University of Utah in 1963. Other researchers at Utah became interested in Winchell's artificial heart, and in 1982, after a few modifications, the first working model was implanted into a patient. One of the Utah team who had worked on the modifications was Dr. Robert Jarvik (b. 1946) who also performed the operation. Jarvik decided to name the artificial heart after himself, and called it the Jarvik-7. Winchell's name was hardly mentioned.

And another thing . . .

One of Paul Winchell's collaborators on the artificial heart project was Dr. Henry Heimlich, who became famous for the "Heimlich Maneuver" for dislodging food stuck in the gullet.

LILLIAN RUSSELL (1860–1922)

Lillian Russell (born Helen Louise Leonard) was one of the most popular American comic actresses and opera singers at the turn of the twentieth century. She was a great beauty and had a famously complicated love life, marrying four times over the course of her life, as well as conducting a large number of extramarital affairs.

Alexander Graham Bell admired the purity of Russell's voice, and chose hers to be the first voice ever transmitted by long-distance telephone.

In 1912, she was granted a patent for an enormous combination dresser-trunk that also doubled as a portable dressing room.

Health

> "God heals. The doctor takes the fees."
>
> **—Benjamin Franklin**

Many of the most important breakthroughs in modern surgery and the treatment of diseases have come from the United States. Some, such as the polio vaccine, have truly changed the world for the better. Others, like Botox, may be more at home on the cosmetics counter.

As of 2007, around $100 billion is spent every year on medical research in the United States, much of it within the U.S. Department of Health and Human Services.

These are some of the most important advances.

BONE-MARROW TRANSPLANT

There was a time when the diagnosis of leukemia was a death sentence. Nowadays bone-marrow transplantation offers a lifeline to many sufferers and stands as one of the most important medical advances of our time. The technique of bone-marrow transplantation is to destroy the diseased bone marrow with near-lethal doses of radiation and chemotherapy, and replace it with healthy new marrow.

The first successful bone-marrow transplant took place in 1956. Since that pioneering operation, tens of thousands of leukemia patients have undergone the same treatment, made a full recovery, and gone on to lead productive lives.

Dr. E. Donnall Thomas (b. 1920) of Cooperstown, New York, performed the operation and went on to win the 1990 Nobel Prize for Physiology or Medicine (jointly awarded to Dr. Joseph E. Murray—see also Kidney Transplant) for his work in the field of cell transplantation.

LIQUID BANDAGE

In 2002, scientists at the University of Utah developed the first liquid bandage. It was a "hydrogel" made up of hyaluronic acid and chondroitin sulphate. Healing rates were improved by 30 percent, and this was partly attributed to the gel's ability to maintain the moistness of the wound.

Often referred to as superglue, because of its cyanoacrylate content, the liquid bandage is increasingly replacing the traditional bandage and sticking plaster. In combat, when wounds require rapid closing, liquid bandage is proving highly effective.

The first liquid bandage approved for the consumer market by the FDA (Food and Drug Administration) was a Johnson & Johnson product and was first marketed in 2002 under the Band-Aid brand. Band-Aid as a form of adhesive bandage was invented by Earle Dickson, an employee of Johnson and Johnson, and was launched in 1921.

BOTOX (BOTULINUM TOXIN)

Botulinum toxin, which is a neurotoxic protein, was first described in a medical paper in the early nineteenth century in Germany, but no good use could be found for it.

In 1980, Dr. Alan Scott of California became the first to use Botox to treat humans. Researchers had found that botulinum toxin was successful in treating muscle spasms. Scott decided to inject a small quantity into the eye muscle of a patient to treat a squint. The treatment was successful, but it would be another nine years before the U.S. Food and Drug Administration officially approved its use in surgery. It is now widely used for treatment of squinting.

Despite botulinum toxin being one of the most toxic naturally occurring substances known to man, the cosmetic use of Botox was approved in 2002.

ANGIOPLASTY

Charles Dotter (1920–1985) is often referred to as the "father of intervention." Intervention is a procedure in which there is minimal invasion of the patient's body, generally by the use of needles or small tubes called catheters.

Dotter is known for his work on the development of angioplasty, the mechanical widening of a blood vessel or vein. The technique is to introduce a tightly packed balloon into the constricted area and inflate it using water pressure. Dotter and his assistant Melvin Judkins first described angioplasty in 1964.

Dotter's greatest contribution was the intervention catheter—a long tube that is fed into the body through a vein. Prior to this invention, all vascular procedures (vascular procedures affect the circulatory system of the body) were done as open surgery involving the patient receiving a general anaesthetic and being opened up for the medical procedure. Recovery from open surgery generally took several days in the hospital. The advantage of the intervention catheter is that it is inserted into the blood vessel, reducing the risks and complications, and the procedure is generally undertaken while the patient is awake.

Dotter's other important work was in the application of arterial stents, which are short tubes inserted into a narrowed artery to hold it open and to assist blood flow.

POLIO VACCINE

Polio (poliomyelitis) is a viral infection that attacks the muscle-controlling nerves of the brain and spinal cord, resulting in paralysis. Most victims are young.

Dr. Jonas Salk

Toward the end of the nineteenth century and during the first half of the twentieth century, a series of major polio epidemics swept through Europe and America, causing the death and paralysis of thousands. Starting in 1910 there was a "great race" to find a vaccine.

There is no cure for the disease, but in 1952, Dr. Jonas Salk (1914–95) discovered a vaccine that would prevent its onset. It was made available to the public on April 12, 1955, and is now widely used for this type of ailment. In a magnificent humane gesture, Salk refused to patent his vaccine, holding that he had no desire to profit personally from his discovery. He wanted only to see the widest possible distribution for the greatest possible good.

IRON LUNG

In 1929, the first polio victim was saved at Brigham Hospital, Boston, using the newly developed Drinker Respirator (iron lung).

The iron lung is a large medical ventilator that consists mainly of a horizontal metal chamber, or drum, in which the patient is placed. Air pressure within the chamber is increased and decreased, which enables the patient to breathe when normal muscle control of the lungs has been lost. Polio victims were treated in iron lungs, although the machine had originally been developed in response to a high incidence of coal gas poisoning. During polio outbreaks in the 1940s and 1950s, hospital wards were filled with patients in iron lungs, but the control of breathing by direct intubation of the airway in modern ventilators has brought about the decline in use of the iron lung.

The inventor of the iron lung was Philip Drinker (1894–1972), who was issued with a patent in 1928. In 1931, a lighter, cheaper, and quieter version was introduced by John Emerson (1906–1997). Drinker entered into an expensive lawsuit against Emerson for patent violations, but it was found that Drinker himself had violated several patents in his own machine. Drinker's patent was promptly declared invalid.

The subsequent success of the Salk vaccine made the iron lung almost obsolete in the treatment of polio.

KIDNEY MACHINE

The artificial kidney, or to give it its proper title, the hemodialysis machine, which is about the size of three standard filing cabinets, was invented in Holland by Willem Kolff (b. 1911) during World War II. The first machine was tested in 1943, and the first life saved in 1945. In the great humanitarian tradition of medical men and women throughout the world, Kolff refused to patent his invention.

Kolff was born in the Netherlands, but moved to the United States in 1950. Some of his most important work took place after his move to the Cleveland Clinic Foundation. While he was at Clevelend, Kolff was involved in the development of the heart-lung machine to maintain breathing functions when the heart is stopped during heart surgery.

Another of Kolff's important projects was the development of the artificial implanted human heart. The artificial heart is designed for critically ill patients who for some reason cannot get a transplant. In 1982, at the University of Utah, Dr. William DeVries implanted the first artificial human heart into a retired dentist, Dr. Barney Clark.

Dr. Clark lived for another 112 days. Since then, a further 350 people have received artificial hearts.

KIDNEY TRANSPLANT

Most surgeons held back from transplanting human organs until the working of the immune system and tissue-matching was better understood. In 1947, Charles Hufnagel (1916–1989) of Brigham Hospital, Boston, in a desperate attempt to save the life of a young woman on the brink of death, transplanted the kidney of a recently deceased person onto her forearm. The young woman was so weak that Hufnagel and his team could not risk moving her, and were forced to operate in her room by the light of a couple of "gooseneck" lamps. The transplanted kidney began to function immediately and gave the patient the vital few days for her own kidneys to recover and begin to function on their own. Happily, she made a full recovery.

The first successful full kidney transplant, in which a donor kidney replaces the patient's own diseased kidney, was performed by Dr. Joseph Murray (b. 1919) in 1954, at the Peter Bent Brigham Hospital in Boston. He took a kidney from Ronald Herrick and transplanted it into his identical twin brother Richard. Richard was dying from chronic nephritis, a kidney disease, and Ronald's donated kidney allowed him to live for another eight years.

Ronald remains alive today, as does Dr. Murray, who was awarded the Nobel Prize for Medicine in 1990.

RUBBER SURGICAL GLOVES

The first surgeon to use rubber gloves while performing an operation was William Halsted of Johns Hopkins Hospital in the USA. In 1889, Halsted had invented the gloves to help prevent medical staff catching dermatitis from surgical chemicals. It was only later that the benefits of rubber gloves in antisepsis were realized.

Halsted, who was the first chief of surgery at the newly opened Johns Hopkins Hospital, is considered by some to be the most influential surgeon ever produced by the United States of America.

BRAIN SURGERY

In 1926, the pioneering brain surgeon Harvey Cushing (1869–1939), who studied under William Halsted (see "Rubber Surgical Gloves"), improved surgical techniques in brain surgery. The new techniques considerably enhanced the chances of a patient's survival after surgery to remove brain tumors.

Cushing was the first to use X-rays to diagnose brain tumors, and was also the first to use electrodes to cauterize (seal by burning) blood vessels during brain surgery.

Cushing is widely regarded as the greatest neurosurgeon of the twentieth century.

STREPTOMYCIN

Streptomycin is an antibiotic drug discovered in 1943 by Albert Schatz (1920–2005) during his research work at Rutgers University in New Jersey.

His supervisor, Selman Waksman (1888–1973), took all the credit for the discovery, and was awarded the Nobel Prize for Medicine in 1952. However, Schatz took out a lawsuit against Waksman, suing him for a share of the streptomycin royalties. Wakman at first contested the claim, but Schatz produced research papers that proved he had done the majority of the work. A substantial out-of-court settlement was made in his favor.

AIDS

AIDS (Acquired Immunodeficiency Syndrome) is a condition in which the body's immune system becomes weakened due to the contraction of the human immunodeficiency virus (HIV). Those infected are susceptible to infections that would be harmless and trivial in most people. In HIV victims, these infections eventually result in death. It is now believed that HIV emerged in the human population quite recently. (Previously, it was an ancestral virus that only infected monkeys.)

AIDS was officially recognized for the first time on June 18, 1981, simultaneously in California and New York. It was originally thought to be a sexually transmitted disease restricted to homosexual men. It was quickly discovered that it could be transmitted to anyone through transfusion of contaminated blood or the use of contaminated intravenous needles or sex. AIDS can also be transmitted from mother to child during pregnancy.

There is currently no cure for either HIV or AIDS, but work in the USA on antiretroviral drugs and PEPS (post-exposure prophylaxis) is proving beneficial to many HIV-infected individuals. After almost thirty years of intensive research, the HIV virus is proving an elusive vaccine target.

The first victim of AIDS through an infected blood transfusion was Don Coffee in 1981 in San Francisco.

HEART SURGERY

Faced with the need to treat high numbers of badly wounded soldiers during World War II, doctors made enormous advances in blood transfusions, anesthetics, and antibiotics. These advances allowed the development of modern surgical practices.

A young U.S. Army surgeon, Dr. Dwight Harken, managed to remove fragments of shrapnel from the hearts of soldiers by inserting his finger into the wound hole, locating the shrapnel, and pulling it out through the same hole in the heart. Harken accomplished this very delicate procedure while the soldiers' hearts were still beating, and it is believed this is the first example of a surgical procedure on live, human hearts.

In 1952, Dr. Bill Bigelow (1913–2005) of the University of Minnesota, who had studied the habits of hibernating animals, had the idea of reducing the patient's temperature from 98 to 81 degrees Fahrenheit. As a result, doctors were able to extend the operating time from four to ten minutes, but it was still an uncomfortably short time in which to do complex procedures.

The first successful hole-in-the-heart operation, to repair a small tear in the inner wall of the heart, was performed on September 2, 1952, by Dr. F. John Lewis and Dr. Walton Lillehei (1918–1999). The patient was a five-year-old girl who had been born with a defective heart. She survived the operation and made a full recovery.

The first successful open-heart surgery took place in Philadelphia on May 15, 1953. Eighteen-year-old college student Cecilia Bavolek had a heart murmur that had been diagnosed as a hole in the wall of her heart. The hole was causing several pints of blood to be shunted back into her lungs every minute, and needed to be closed up. She was connected to Dr. Gibbon's heart-lung machine for forty-five minutes, and for twenty-seven of those minutes, the machine breathed for her and pumped her blood. Dr. Gibbon, who also performed the operation, was able to open Cecelia's heart and stitch together the hole that had appeared between two of the auricles.

This was the first time a heart had been operated on in a dry (bloodless) condition.

HEART-LUNG MACHINE

In 1953, Dr. John Gibbon Jr. (1903–1973) of Philadelphia developed the heart-lung machine. This very complex machine duplicated the work of both organs during operations in which the heart had to be stopped, and it overcame the difficulty of keeping the brain supplied with blood during open-heart surgery. It allowed the heart to be kept in a resting condition for the operation so that the surgeon had sufficient time to perform complex procedures.

Dr. Gibbon had worked extensively on his machine for many years and had progressed to the point that in 1949 the heart section worked well on dogs, but was not yet ready for use on humans. The problem was that in order to maintain an adequate supply of oxygen to the blood being pumped by the heart section, a replacement for the human lung was required. By 1953 Dr. Gibbon was satisfied that the newly-developed lung section of the machine would work effectively, and was ready to be put into use.

In Dr. Gibbon's machine, one pump drew in the blood, and another sped it to the oxygen chamber, where it flowed over a set of metal grids, which looked rather like the plates in a storage battery. The metal grids assisted in the oxygenation of the blood. A third pump sent the freshly oxygenated blood back to the heart. In between, the flow rate of the blood was maintained at the correct level by a set of electronic controls.

OPEN-HEART SURGERY

In open-heart surgery, the surgeon performs an operation on the inside of a human heart in which he or she has made an incision. The problem the surgeon faces is that the heart must be stopped to perform the surgery. Once the heart is stopped, the surgeon has only four minutes to complete the operation. Any longer and the patient's brain would be irreparably damaged due to lack of oxygenated blood pumped by the heart.

ROBOTICS

One of the most exciting areas of modern medicine, which is currently gaining wider acceptance, is the introduction of robotic assistance. This operating technique developed out of the need to control the greater hand tremors experienced when surgeons are conducting operations using minimally invasive surgery.

In traditional heart surgery, the chest is opened and the surgeon is able to put his hands physically inside the chest cavity to make incisions close to the organ itself. In minimally invasive surgery that avoids major incisions, the incision may be no bigger than a few millimeters long. The instruments are introduced into the body from a location other than the inside of the incision, and are therefore much longer. This added length leads to normal hand tremors being magnified.

Using robotic assistance, the surgeon is also able to conduct the operation from a remote location—even from another country.

The first robot-assisted heart-bypass operations were performed in late 1998. Dr. Ralph Damiano treated seventeen patients at Pennsylvania State Hospital.

CYBERKNIFE

The CyberKnife is a robotic radio surgery system capable of delivering controlled doses of radiotherapy with pinpoint accuracy. It is mainly used in the treatment of tumors. The device was invented by John Adler (b. 1954), a Stanford University Professor of Neurosurgery and Radiation Oncology.

Radiation is produced in a small, linear particle accelerator in the CyberKnife, and it is capable of accepting very precise surgical instructions. This enables it to treat tumors in difficult to reach parts of the body, as the energy can be directed to any part of the body by remote control.

Crime

> "But treason is not owned when 'tis descried;
> Successful crimes alone are justified."
> **—John Dryden** (1631–1700)

American crime and criminals have fascinated the rest of the world since the era of the great Hollywood crime melodramas. American gangsters somehow seem more romantic, the crimes more daring and successful than anywhere else. Edward G. Robinson, George Raft, and James Cagney, with their trademark strutting and snarling, seemed to embody the gangster as tough-guy hero. Books and films about the Mafia, particularly the Mario Puzo books, beginning with *The Godfather*, did nothing to dampen the appetite for more American crime. On the contrary, the world's appetite wanted to be fed, and fed it was.

Lurid stories have filled the newspapers about the real-life American underworld, with its loyalties to family and gang, its massacres, its tentacles stretching into everyday life, and its control over the judiciary and even the government. Stories such as these have reinforced overseas opinion that crime in the United States is bigger and somehow better than any small-fry homegrown version.

Before the USA became an independent nation in 1776 and introduced federal laws, the law was enforced on a city-by-city basis, with each city adopting its own legal system. The severity of the punishments relied to a large degree on the prevailing circumstances in the city and the attitude of the city fathers.

The first Night Watch in the United States, which was established in Boston in 1631, was set up to guard private property during the hours of darkness. Slave Patrols, which were set up to look for runaway slaves, were instituted in the southern states in 1704. These were the forerunners of U.S. police forces.

U.S. Marshals were first appointed in 1789, under the Federal Judiciary Act, and in 1823 the Texas Rangers were formed to protect settlers from hostile Indian attacks. At the time, Texas was part of Mexico and would remain Mexican until 1836.

The first unified, prevention-oriented police force in the USA was established in New York City in 1845, but uniforms were not issued until 1853.

Allan Pinkerton (1819–1884) established the Pinkerton Detective Agency in 1850. His inspiration came after success as an amateur in locating the hideout of a counterfeiting gang that had eluded capture by official forces. Pinkerton was a Scottish barrel maker who had emigrated to the USA in 1842 and settled close to Chicago.

The forerunner of the FBI (Federal Bureau of Investigations) was a force known as the Special Agents, which was set up in 1908 under the leadership of Attorney General Charles Bonaparte (1851–1921). Bonaparte had a colorful background as the grandson of Jerome Bonaparte, the youngest brother of the French Emperor, Napoleon I. He began operations with just thirty-four agents. At the time, there were only a handful of federal crimes on the statute book, which included antitrust, land, and banking frauds.

ORGANIZED CRIME
Chinese Tongs

During the 1840s and 1850s, the Asian community in the USA, made up principally of Chinese immigrants, experienced racist treatment by whites. In response, the Chinese population in Chicago formed a visible community, and it was within this "Chinatown" that gang activity first began. Tong gangs were established as merchants' associations, and organized to protect members' interests.

Contrary to popular myth, Tong gangs are virtually unheard of in China.

Mafia (a.k.a. Cosa Nostra)

Since its establishment in the USA, the Mafia has become the most notorious and powerful criminal organization in the world. It was established as a secret organization in Sicily in the late Middle Ages, and was originally formed to overthrow the rule of foreign conquerors such as the Saracens, Normans, and Spanish.

The Mafia originated through small, private armies (*mafie*), hired by absentee landlords to protect their estates. Over time these armies became very powerful, and in the eighteenth and nineteenth centuries began to extort money from their previous employers.

It was sometimes referred to as the Black Hand Gang, after its signature of a black handprint left at the scene of a murder. This practice fell into disuse after the establishment of fingerprinting.

The Mafia survived successive foreign governments. It also flourished despite the efforts of the Italian dictator Benito Mussolini (1883–1945), who came closest to eliminating the organization by the application of repressive methods as harsh as those used by the Mafia itself. During Mussolini's appointment of Cesare Mori (1871–1942) as the prefect of Palermo, there were over one 1,000 gangland arrests on the island. Mori was under instruction to use any method he chose to defeat the Mafia. He was not above taking women and children as hostages to hold as bargaining chips against gang members. After his recall to Rome in 1929, it was announced that the Mafia had been defeated.

It was a premature announcement.

During the great nineteenth century waves of Sicilian immigration into the USA, criminal gangs quickly established themselves on the East Coast and in Chicago, and some of the early characters have passed into legend—men like "Big" Jim Colossimo, Johnny Torio, and Antonio Lombardo.

The great rebirth of the Mafia came after World War II when it transferred its powers and interests from the rural to the great industrial areas, and began an underworld invasion of the United States. By the 1950s the Mafia had come to dominate organized crime in the USA, and although its traditional home was Sicily, the real power base was America. From there the families that made up the American Mafia grew to control a world empire of crime, their grip as powerful as a state of war.

The first Capo di Tutti Capi (Boss of Bosses), was "Lucky" Luciano (1896–1962). In 1934, he united crime families from cities around the USA in a common purpose by creating the National Crime Syndicate. He was able to do this through alliances with Meyer Lansky (1902–1983) and "Bugsy" Siegel (1906–1947), his boyhood friends and fellow gangsters.

Ku Klux Klan

The origin of the name of the Ku Klux Klan is uncertain, but one theory maintains that the name comes from the Greek word *kuklos*, meaning wheel, and *klan*, meaning family.

The first Ku Klux Klan had six members, who met on Christmas Eve 1865 in a law office in Pulaski, Tennessee, supposedly with the intention of forming a social group devoted to wearing weird costumes and playing practical jokes on unsuspecting people. By the end of 1866, in the wake of the American Civil War, its activities had spread beyond Tennessee and progressed to real violence. The violence was aimed at intimidating freedmen—the 4 million former slaves who had been emancipated with the defeat of the southern states.

In 1867 the Ku Klux Klan appointed its first Grand Wizard, the former Confederate General Nathan Forrest (1821–1877), with the backing of former Confederate leader General Robert E. Lee (1807–1870). Some of the other original ranks were Grand Dragon, Titan, Giant, Grand Cyclops, and Ghoul (the lowest rank).

In 1868, the Ku Klux Klan was blamed for up to 1,300 murders. This first version of the Klan was disbanded in 1869.

The second Ku Klux Klan was formed in 1915 by William J. Simmons (b. 1880), who set down the prospectus of the organization while he was recovering in hospital from a car-accident injury. Simmons's thinking was strongly influenced by the D. W. Griffith film *The Birth of a Nation*, also known as *The Clansman*. The re-formation of the Klan was marked by the burning of a cross on Stone Mountain in Atlanta, Georgia, on November 25, 1915.

This second version of the KKK was a deeply sinister organization, bent on serious, racially motivated crime. It is said that at the peak of its activities in the 1920s, membership reached almost 4 million men. By the late 1930s, membership was in terminal decline, and in 1939, the Grand Wizard, Hiram Evans, sold the organization to James Colecutt, an Indiana veterinarian. Facing an immense tax bill from the Internal Revenue Service, the second version of the Ku Klux Klan was dissolved in 1944.

Several minor versions of the Klan have existed since those days and in 2005 it was estimated that there were approximately 2,500 members.

CAPITAL PUNISHMENT

Lethal Injection

Lethal injection as a form of capital punishment raises ethical questions separate from the debate over the morality of capital punishment itself. This is the only procedure that mimics hospital conditions and involves the participation of a doctor as executioner.

Lethal injection was first proposed by Dr. J. Mount Bleyer of New York in 1888 as a humanitarian means of execution, but it was not used in the USA for almost a century, until Charles Brooks's execution in Texas on December 7, 1982.

Dr. Stanley Deutsch, an anesthetist at the University of Oklahoma, formulated the contents of the modern lethal injection in 1977. He recommended an intravenous infusion of a barbiturate followed by a muscle relaxant as an "ideal and inexpensive way of bringing about a speedy and very humane demise."

Electric Chair

The idea for the electric chair came from an American dentist named Albert Southwick in 1881. Southwick had witnessed the instant death in the street of an elderly drunk who accidentally touched the terminals of an electricity generator.

The first execution by alternating current electric chair was of the axe-murderer William Kemmler in 1890 in New York's Auburn State Prison. The chair had been invented by Dr. J. Mount Bleyer, the man who had earlier proposed lethal injections. The whole event was a shambles, with the condemned man suffering a horrible, lingering death instead of the instant death that had been anticipated.

The public outcry over Kemmler's final agony played into the hands of Thomas Edison, who had a business manufacturing the far more lethal, direct-current electric chairs.

Gas Chamber

The gas chamber was invented in 1924 by Major Delos A. Turner of the U.S. Army Medical Corps, as a supposedly humane means of executing people. It turned out to be the very opposite, as the process turned out to take more than nine minutes. Several examples of the process lasted over twenty minutes.

The first execution by gas chamber took place in Nevada on February 8, 1924. Mr. Gee Jong was executed for a murder that was linked to a Tong war. Jong's accomplice, Hughie Sing, was also sentenced to death, but this sentence was later commuted to life imprisonment.

Eaton Metal Products of Salt Lake City had almost a complete U.S. monopoly on gas-chamber manufacture.

Lynching

The form of execution known as lynching refers to the concept of vigilantism in which citizens, in the form of a mob, illegally assume the roles of prosecutor, judge, jury, and executioner. Defense is not permitted.

The term lynch is derived from the name of Colonel Charles Lynch (1736–1796) a Virginia landowner, who began to hold illegal trials in his backyard in 1790. The accused was rounded up by Lynch's vigilantes, put on summary trial, normally found guilty, then immediately tied to a tree and whipped by Lynch. In some cases he would seize property, coerce a pledge of allegiance, or even administer the death penalty by hanging.

Writing to Col. William Preston in 1780, Lynch tries to justify his abhorrent behavior:

Dr Sr

I was honour'd with yours a few days past in which you desire me to desist in trying torys &c &c—What sort of trials you have been informed I have given them I know not, but I can assure you that I only examine them strictly & such as I believe not very criminal I set at liberty. Others I have for a proper trial, some I have kept for soldiers, some as witnesses, some perhaps Justice of the County may require that shou'd be made examples of…I would also request the favour of you let me have a sight of letters you receiv'd relative to my conduct &c &c.

Some nineteenth-century writers began to sentimentalize Lynch's murderous violence and ethnic prejudices, but documentary proof now clearly shows the extent of his activities.

The first victim in America of this summary form of justice was John Billington in 1630. He had arrived in America on the *Mayflower* in 1620 as a pilgrim, and was the prime suspect when his neighbor, John Newcomen, was shot. He was summarily hanged by a mob of other pilgrims.

CRIME

The majority of lynchings in the USA took part between 1880 and 1930, in most cases the result of racial hatred in the southern states. Of the 2,800 known victims, 2,500 were black. Ida Wells (1862–1931), an African American journalist who had been born into slavery, wrote in the *Chicago Defender* that as many as 10,000 people were probably lynched between 1879 and 1898.

The Anti-Lynching Bill was first proposed in 1900 and was passed by the House of Representatives in 1922. Its passage to approval was delayed by a number of filibusters and the Senate finally approved the bill in June 2005 with a formal apology for its failure to approve it earlier.

FICTIONAL DETECTIVES

Sam Spade

Sam Spade was first featured in 1922 in stories Dashiell Hammett wrote for the *Black Mask* magazine. Humphrey Bogart was perfectly cast in this hard-bitten role in the 1941 film *The Maltese Falcon*.

Philip Marlowe

Philip Marlowe first appeared in the 1939 novel *The Big Sleep* by Raymond Chandler (1888–1959). In the 1946 film based on the book, Humphrey Bogart (1899–1957) provided the definitive performance of Marlowe, starring alongside his future wife, Lauren Bacall (b. 1924).

Marlowe has a tough, hard-drinking, wisecracking outer shell that hides a contemplative side, easily drawn to poetry and philosophy, and with a strong moral sense.

Criminals

If criminals could ever be called glamorous, those American criminals of the Jazz Age and the American Prohibition era would qualify. They were mostly vicious thugs with serious sociopathic tendencies, but their exploits were reported in such exotic detail that even the most skeptical reader would somehow link their lifestyles to that of Robin Hood. The most famous of them all, Al Capone, made as many headlines as the great sporting idols of the time. His picture was taken quite openly, by press photographers, alongside genuine public heroes like Babe Ruth, and he was always ready with a pithy quote for any nearby newshound. The public lapped up the sensational stories, and his was the almost-acceptable face of crime. When asked at a party how he justified selling beer and liquor, he said, "All I'm doing lady, is satisfying a need."

Capone dominated the streets and speakeasies of 1920s and 1930s Chicago, wearing a white fedora and smoking a fat cigar. He looked like a movie star or a producer, but he was responsible for hundreds of deaths and millions of crimes. In his own time, and for the more than sixty years since his death, his name has been synonymous with the business he so dominated.

Organized crime is now a more secretive business. The bosses avoid publicity at all costs, or at least the successful ones do. They believe there is nothing, apart from self-aggrandizement, to be gained by having your name in the news. The men who run the major crime syndicates are serious businessmen and see all publicity as bad for business. It has not always been this way, and the names of the infamous come readily to mind.

Alongside the mobsters and their bosses are some other singularly evil men and women. Their names have captured the attention of newsrooms around the world. Their pictures have dominated the front pages of foreign papers in a way that the criminals of other countries never do. Who could name a French crook, a Japanese mob boss or a British train robber? Few people outside their own countries could name any foreign criminal, but American criminals' names are known around the world.

Here are some of the best known.

AL "SCARFACE" CAPONE

Alphonse Gabriel Capone (1899–1947) was born and grew up in Brooklyn, New York before moving to Chicago to pursue his life of crime. By his late twenties he was a worldwide celebrity.

Al Capone

In perhaps the best book written about this creature of myth and violence, Fred Pasley introduces his subject by saying, "Al Capone was to crime what J. P. Morgan was to Wall Street, the first man to exert national influence over his trade." Others have compared him to John D. Rockefeller of Standard Oil as the clear leader of his industry.

When Capone first came to Chicago in 1920, the city was split into two groups of rival criminal gangs. Capone first took over the gang Johnny Torio had built in the city, and then he ruthlessly eliminated the opposition. He moved on to control the city suburbs, extended his reach further to control crime in the whole state of Illinois and then, in 1929, called the first international gangland convention at Atlantic City. As the strongest among the leaders at the convention, Capone was able to carve the whole country into territories with precisely marked borders for each of the major gangs. Crime had reached the stage of oligopoly and the small-time criminal was nearly eliminated. The gangs actually cooperated with the police to get rid of them, and according to some observers, in this sense the crime syndicate played a positive role for society.

At the height of his power in the 1920s, Capone had a personal income greater than $60 million per year, and most of it had been earned because of the Volstead Act, the constitutional amendment that prohibited the sale of alcohol. What the politicians failed to understand was that Prohibition would not quench the public's thirst for beer, liquor, wine, and a good time.

Into the vacuum caused by the departure of legitimate business stepped the criminal gangs. Capone ended up owning breweries throughout Illinois and running truckloads of liquor across the border with Canada, south to his warehouses. His ruthlessness and organizing skills were legendary, and it was thought even at the time that he could have made his pile in legitimate business had he not been born in a place where the only way to fortune seemed to be through crime.

Rivals were eliminated in craven massacres, police chiefs were ignored or bought off and it was said that judges were only appointed once Capone had approved them. The famous "Untouchables" led by Eliot Ness were the only visible threat to his empire. They seriously dented (but in the end were not able to close down) Capone's operations.

> "You can get more with a nice word and a gun than you can with just a nice word."
>
> **—Al Capone**

Capone was arrested more than once but he was never convicted of his crimes. In 1931 he was found guilty of tax evasion and sentenced to eleven years in jail. After release he was never the same, and died of complications from syphilis at the age of forty-eight, a gibbering wreck of the man that had once ruled the world of crime.

> "Prohibition has made nothing but trouble."
>
> **—Al Capone**

ALBERT "THE MAD HATTER" ANASTASIA

Albert Anastasia (1902–1957) was a brutal thug who became famous for running the contract homicide gang known as Murder, Inc. during the 1940s. He rose to his place after acting as a hired killer for "Lucky" Luciano, and for helping to eliminate Luciano's rivals.

In 1957, Anastasia was murdered while he sat in the barber's chair at the Park Sheraton Hotel on 7th Avenue in New York City, in a classic gangland execution. Two masked gunmen burst into the shop and opened fire at close range. Anastasia was not killed outright but lunged mistakenly for his killers' reflections in a side mirror before finally slumping to the floor. No bystanders were hurt, but the papers had a glorious time showing graphic photos of the bloody results of the execution.

The killers have never been brought to justice, but there are strong suspicions that the major gang bosses colluded to have him "rubbed out."

JACK "LEGS" DIAMOND

Legs Diamond (1897–1931) was an Irish American gangster during the Prohibition Era, in New York. He was known as the "clay pigeon of the underworld," having survived several attempts on his life.

During service in the U.S. Army in 1919, Diamond deserted. He was arrested and jailed. After his release he joined a criminal gang and quickly progressed to become a kidnapper and murderer. He led a flamboyant lifestyle and became a major celebrity in New York. It is said that he acquired the nickname "Legs" because he was such a good dancer.

Diamond's bootlegging activity brought him into conflict with the implacable "Dutch" Shultz, the local gang boss.

Big mistake.

In 1931, Diamond was shot in the head three times as he left a Christmas party. It was always thought the execution was the work of the Schultz gang, but rumors persisted that it could even have been a police setup.

Years passed with no leads, but in a 1974 interview, the local Democratic Party chairman Dan O'Connell confirmed that it had not been the Schultz gang who executed Legs Diamond, but the local police chief. After that revelation it was speculated that O'Connell himself had held such a grip on local crime, and such power over the police, that he would not allow any intruders to gain a foothold. Legs Diamond paid the price for not looking after the right people.

GEORGE CLARENCE "BUGS" MORAN (born ADELARD CUNIN)

Bugs Moran (1891–1957) was born in St Paul, Minnesota, but moved to Chicago in his late teens.

Chicago was at that time roughly divided between Irish gangs in the north (the North Side gang) and Italians in the south (the South Side gang). In the late 1920s, Moran's bootlegging activities were not only posing challenges to Al Capone's business, but Moran had begun to insult Capone in the press, calling him "Scarface" and the "behemoth." He also made two serious attempts on Capone's life and murdered his bodyguard after torturing him with hot wires.

A great deal of bad blood existed between the two men, with each of them staging robberies of the other's goods. Capone burned down

Moran's dog track and Moran retaliated by burning down one of Capone's clubs. In an effort to strike a decisive blow, Capone arranged to ambush Moran at one of his warehouses. He sent in armed men dressed as police officers who gunned down almost the whole gang. It was immortalized as the "St. Valentine's Day Massacre" and grabbed headlines around the world. Moran himself managed to avoid the mayhem. He had spotted what he assumed was a police patrol car waiting outside his building and sat in a local café to await events. Capone had missed his main target.

In 1946, Moran was arrested for robbing a bank messenger and was sentenced to ten years in jail. He received a further ten years for a previous robbery and was sent to Leavenworth.

Bugs Moran died of lung cancer in the prison hospital. The man who had challenged Capone himself, and who was worth millions of dollars at the pinnacle of his criminal career, was estimated to be worth no more than $100 at his death.

FRANK COSTELLO (born FRANK CASTIGLIA)

Frank Costello (1891–1973) rose to the top of the crime world, controlling a vast gambling, prostitution, and drug-trafficking empire. With his friend and business partner Lucky Luciano, he teamed up with other criminal leaders in New York, and between them they became involved in robberies, extortion, and narcotics.

After a bloody and wasteful intergang war, Luciano emerged as "Capo" (boss). After he was framed in a rape case and jailed for thirty to fifty years, Luciano appointed Costello as acting boss of the Luciano crime family. At the end of World War II, Luciano was deported to Sicily, leaving Costello as undisputed boss of the family.

A rival, Vito Genovese, began to challenge for the top job, and life became very dangerous for Costello. After several attempts on his life he did an unheard-of thing for a gang boss: he retired. He managed to retain a few small criminal interests in Florida and Louisiana.

He finally died in a hospital at the age of eighty-two.

CARLO "DON CARLO" GAMBINO

Carlo Gambino (1902–1976) never saw the inside of a prison and once he had achieved a position of power, didn't feel the need to carry

Carlo Gambino
in later life

a gun. He was a dedicated family man, and as likely to fetch a photo of one of his grandchildren out of his pocket to show people, as to discuss business.

Gambino was the only New York crime boss bold enough to attend the funeral of his old friend Lucky Luciano. After the burial, he made a speech which established him as the undisputed Boss of Bosses (Capo di Tutti Capi) in New York. He expanded his rackets all over America, and despite twenty-four-hour surveillance by the FBI, who used wiretaps, lip readers, and cameras, Gambino was able to control his empire in silence. At the end of a day's eavesdropping, the FBI's recording tapes would invariably be empty, except for Gambino occasionally asking for a cup of coffee.

He died of a heart attack at home in 1976, but the crime syndicate he ruled—the Gambino family—retains his name.

VITO GENOVESE

Vito "Don Vito" Genovese (1897–1969) began his criminal career in the USA in the 1920s. In 1937 he was indicted on a murder charge and fled to Italy.

After American troops invaded Naples in 1944, Genovese acted as an interpreter and liaison officer, dealing with the local population. At the same time, he was running an immense black-market operation. He was arrested on charges of black-market trading, and eventually returned to New York, where he also had to face the murder charge he had run away from in 1937.

The charges failed and Genovese returned to his old gang, the Luciano family, but only as an underboss. He was not happy. He saw this as a demotion and in a bloody series of attacks he disposed of all who stood in his way—Albert Anastasia, Willie Moretti, Anthony Strollo, and Anthony Carfano. He seized control of the Luciano family and appointed his own people to the top jobs.

In 1957, Genovese called together dozens of Mafiosi to a conference in Apalachin, New York. A local state trooper had been watching the house where they all gathered. They had chosen the home of a local mobster—big mistake. When the policeman saw the group of known crooks gathering in one place, he called in reinforcements. The police arrived and the gangsters scattered in a chaotic panic, running in all directions. Some ran into the local woods.

Two years later Genovese was sentenced to fifteen years in jail for a narcotics offense. Rumors circulated that the police had finally had enough and planted the drugs.

He died of a heart attack in a prison hospital in 1969.

CHARLES "LUCKY" LUCIANO

Lucky Luciano (1897–1962) was that rarity among gangsters, a master strategist and organizer. Like Capone, Luciano was able to see the big picture, plan well ahead, and execute his plans with coldhearted efficiency.

He is given credit for being the creator of modern organized crime in America and his name is a byword for the tough, cunning, gang boss. His legacy is such that he was named in *Time* magazine among the twenty most influential people of the twentieth century.

Luciano's criminal career started early; he was still in his teens when he was sent to jail for six months for a narcotics offense. Through the Prohibition era, he made his first major fortune. In 1919 he began importing Scotch whiskey directly from Scotland and rum from the Caribbean. He operated a massive bootlegging operation, extending well outside of New York, and by the end of Prohibition he had risen to become a major player in the crime world. Through much plotting and many assassinations he finally made it to the top of the pile and in 1931 he became the de facto *Capo di Tutti Capi*. He refused to have this as official recognition, and abolished the title. He felt it set up jealousies within the criminal world and led to murder bids, which were generally bad for business.

Luciano's masterstroke was to set up The Commission—effectively the court of last appeal for gangsters and the ruling body of organized crime in America. He was soon singled out by the FBI for prosecution, and was sentenced to thirty to fifty years for running a prostitution ring. He continued to run his organization from prison and was rumored to have helped the Allied cause during World War II through his mafia connections in Sicily.

Luciano collapsed and died at Naples International Airport while waiting to meet a movie producer who planned to make a film of his life.

MEYER LANSKY

Meyer Lansky (1902–1983) was instrumental, together with Lucky Luciano, in setting up The Commission, the ruling body of the Mafia families in the United States.

Although he was Jewish, and therefore seen as an outsider not to be fully trusted, Lansky was invaluable in the development of the Italian Mafia businesses. He headed up Murder, Inc and was one of the biggest players in the development of Las Vegas.

At the age of eighty, Lansky died of lung cancer.

FRANK "THE ENFORCER" NITTI

Francesco Raffaele Nitto (1888–1943) was one of Al Capone's chief henchmen. After Capone was jailed, Nitti ran the "Chicago Mob" as his front man, although others are known to have wielded the real power in the organization. Nitti's name came more into public prominence in the 1960s TV series, *The Untouchables*, when he was portrayed as a tough thug (although in real life he was more of a planner than an action man).

Nitti planned the wholesale extortion of the movie industry. Studios such as MGM, Paramount, Twentieth Century Fox, and Columbia were threatened with union action if they failed to pay protection money. It all went horribly wrong as an informer exposed the racket. Nitti's accomplices wanted him to "take the rap" and he faced jail time. On the day before his scheduled appearance before the Grand Jury, Nitti shot himself in the head. As he was only using a .32 caliber weapon, it took him several shots to do the deed.

BENJAMIN "BUGSY" SIEGEL

Bugsy Siegel (1906–1947) was heavily involved in the large-scale development of Las Vegas.

Siegel's life in crime began alongside all the major Italian criminal figures of the Prohibition era. He formed associations with Luciano, Costello, and Lansky and was eventually sent to the Nevada Desert to oversee the development of the first major casino, The Flamingo. Through incompetence and bribery, construction ran massively over budget and Siegel was shot in the head as he sat in the home of a friend in Beverley Hills, Los Angeles.

"DUTCH" SHULTZ (real name ARTHUR FLEGENHEIMER)

Dutch Schultz (1902–1935) was a rarity among gangsters of the Prohibition era. He was neither Sicilian nor Italian. He made a name for himself as a brutal thug when crossed, and established himself in New York, extorting restaurants, and running several different rackets. He was beginning to get out of control.

Schultz is most famous for storming out of a meeting of The Commission after they had unanimously voted that he should not go ahead with his planned assassination of Thomas Dewey, the special prosecutor who had had arraigned Schultz for tax evasion. The members rightly forecast that the FBI would be brought in if an attorney were to be murdered.

Fearing that Schultz would go ahead with the killing in defiance of the order, his own murder was arranged. As he stood at the urinal in a restaurant in Newark, New Jersey, two men burst in and shot him in the abdomen. The bullets were covered in rust to ensure that Schultz would die of poison if the shots failed to finish him off. He died twenty-two hours later in hospital.

> "The chimney sweeps. Talk to the sword. Shut up you got a big mouth! Please help me up Henry. Max, come over here. French-Canadian bean soup. I want to pay. Let them leave me alone."
> **—the deathbed words of Dutch Schultz,**
> as taken down by the police stenographer.

JOHN GOTTI (a.k.a. THE TEFLON DON)

John Joseph Gotti (1940–2002) became boss of the powerful Gambino family in New York after the murder of Paul Castellano, his former boss.

John Gotti

Gotti was called the "Teflon Don" because of his ability to avoid arrest. His flamboyant lifestyle led to publicity in the press. It also caused his eventual conviction for murder, extortion, conspiracy to murder, illegal gambling, and loan sharking. He was sentenced to life.

He was a short-tempered, brutal man who did not restrict himself to violence within the organization, but regularly beat his own family. He is said to have used a chainsaw to personally dismember the man who had accidentally run over and killed his youngest son.

Like many other mob bosses, Gotti died early, although in his case it was not from violence. He had served ten years of his life sentence when he died in the prison hospital of throat cancer.

BONNIE and CLYDE

Bonnie Parker (1910–1934) and Clyde Barrow (1909–1934) were notorious outlaws who robbed banks, gas stations, and small stores in an orgy of activity during the Great Depression.

The press ran a series of sensational stories about the pair, and the American public thrilled to read of their exploits. They were thought of as modern-day Robin Hood characters. The truth is less attractive. Nine police officers lost their lives during their robberies, as well as several bystanders.

The pair was gunned down in a police ambush of their car on May 23, 1934. Police emptied around 130 rounds of ammunition into the car and both died on the spot. Such was their reputation that the police, not wanting to take any chances, used shotguns, pistols, rifles, and even automatic rifles.

The Bonnie and Clyde story has been told on screen three times, most notably in the romanticized 1967 film starring Warren Beatty and Faye Dunaway.

JOHN DILLINGER

John Herbert Dillinger (1903–1934) was a bank robber who caught the popular imagination during the Great Depression. He was known as "The Jack Rabbit" from his trademark athletic leap over the bank counter during a robbery.

Dillinger was widely reported in the press for his sheer cheek. One of his more adventurous exploits was to pose as a bank alarm system salesman. He entered several banks in this guise and had free rein to assess their security. He would come back later to relieve them of their cash. Another trick he used was to have his gang pose as a film crew scouting for scenes for a bank robbery. When the actual robbery took place, bystanders would stand around thinking it was all part of the movie.

Dillinger met his death while leaving the Biograph Theater in Lincoln Park, Chicago. He was "fingered" by the famous Woman in Red, a brothel-keeper known as Anna Sage. She agreed with the FBI to wear the dress (it was actually orange but showed up red under the theater lights) as a means of identifying him. He suspected something was wrong and made a run for it, drawing his gun as he fled, but he was struck in the back of the head by a bullet and died on the spot.

Controversy followed Dillinger even after his death. For several years it was thought that the wrong man had been killed. Even Dillinger's father, on seeing the corpse exclaimed, "That's not my son!" Later forensic evidence was assembled that established that the dead man was in fact John Dillinger.

JESSE JAMES

Jesse Woodson James (1847–1882) became a legendary figure of the "Wild West" through his outlaw activities. His fame spread abroad despite the fact that he only conducted his criminal activities within a small area of the United States.

Jesse James

James's home state of Missouri was ripped apart during the American Civil War. Guerrilla warfare had taken hold during the conflict, with an infamous gang called Quantrill's Raiders leading most of the activity. At one time James was wrongly thought to be a member of Quantrill's Raiders. After the war, the guerrilla raiders carried on with their raids, but this time with monetary gain as their main objective. Jesse James turned outlaw by joining them and began to rob trains.

The press had a field day reporting his exploits and as he almost never robbed passengers, only the onboard safe, he attained a Robin Hood status. The rail companies were less amused and engaged the services of the Pinkerton Detective Agency. Allan Pinkerton himself took James's run of successful robberies as a personal insult, and appointed himself to bring Jesse James to face the law.

With the number of James's raids escalating, and a foiled bank raid in 1876 in which innocent bystanders were killed, a massive manhunt was put into action. The so-called James/Younger gang was broken up.

James was shot in the back of the head by a fellow gang member, Robert Ford, who tried unsuccessfully to claim the reward of $5,000. The press again sensationalized Jesse James's death and Ford was branded as a coward for shooting James in the back of the head.

BUTCH CASSIDY and THE SUNDANCE KID

Butch Cassidy (real name Robert LeRoy Parker) (1866–1908) achieved notoriety as the leader of the Hole-in-the-Wall gang, which robbed trains and banks.

His life of crime began in 1880 and ended with his biggest robbery in 1905, which took place in Argentina. In between, he teamed up with Henry Longabaugh (the Sundance Kid) (1867–1908). Their exploits were popularized in the 1969 film starring Robert Redford and the late, great Paul Newman.

Butch Cassidy

The Sundance Kid and his girlfriend, Etta Place

As the law was beginning to catch up with them, they found fewer and fewer places to hide in the United States. Traveling on a British steamer going south, they wound up in South America.

The facts surrounding the deaths of Cassidy and The Kid are uncertain. According to the records, both were shot and killed in a gunfight with local officials in Bolivia. However, rumors spread that both survived and went on to live anonymous lives, occasionally visiting friends and family until about 1937 or 1938. Reliable witnesses have stated that Cassidy continued to be treated by his doctor, a woman of absolute integrity, for many years after his reported death.

PRETTY BOY FLOYD

Charles Arthur Floyd (1904–1934) robbed banks and killed people. His first recorded crime was the stealing of $3.50 from a post office in 1922.

After he had robbed the payroll at one particular company, the payroll master described him as "a pretty boy with apple cheeks." His nickname was born. The press loved it. Floyd hated it.

The folk singer Woody Guthrie romanticized Floyd in his 1939 song "The Ballad of Pretty Boy Floyd." It had the effect of perpetuating Floyd's name, and making him out to be something of a hero.

On October 22, 1934, Floyd was killed in a police ambush. There are conflicting accounts of the facts. Some accounts attribute his death to the FBI and others to the local police. One account states that he was shot by an officer, under direct orders from his chief, at point-blank range after he had been captured and was already unarmed.

Such was Floyd's popularity in his home state of Oklahoma, resulting from his generosity to the poor, that around 20,000 people attended his funeral.

BABY FACE NELSON

Lester Joseph Gillis (1908–1934) (a.k.a. Baby Face Nelson) stood only 5'3" tall and robbed banks.

In the 1920s Nelson had a brief time with Al Capone's Chicago Mob, but it didn't last long due mainly to Nelson's hair-trigger temper and his tendency to shoot first and ask questions later. He was jailed in 1931 but escaped and began a series of bank robberies. In 1933, he joined the Dillinger gang, but unlike the Robin Hood style of Pretty Boy Floyd, which the press had so successfully popularized, Nelson's image was that of a vicious killer who would not hesitate to mow down innocent bystanders. At least twelve law officers met their deaths at the hands of Baby Face Nelson.

In a strange twist of fate, he died after an unnecessary gun battle. It became known as The Battle of Barrington. As he was driving along a road with his wife, he spotted two law officers driving in the opposite direction. He decided to turn around and give chase. After he had stopped their car, a shootout began in which machine guns were used. Both officers were killed and Nelson himself received seventeen bullet wounds. He died later that night. His wife wrapped his body in a blanket and left it at the side of the road in a ditch.

Unlike many others, Nelson, who was only twenty-five when he died, was not mourned by the public.

JOHN WILKES BOOTH

In one of the pivotal tragedies of the American national story, John Wilkes Booth (1838–1865) shot and killed Abraham Lincoln (1809–1865). Lincoln is widely recognized as one of the greatest men to have served as president of the United States of America. His words, repeated often, as he heard that General Robert E. Lee had surrendered on April 9 1865, and that the American Civil War was over were, "I've never been so glad in my life." His happiness lasted only a few short days. On April 14, 1865, he was shot in the theater by John Wilkes Booth and died the following morning.

On the morning after the assassination, a posse of 2,000 men galloped out of Washington in pursuit of Booth, who had escaped into the night. Twelve days later, a detachment of twenty-five of the soldiers tracked him and an accomplice to a tobacco barn in Port Royal, Virginia. The accomplice soon surrendered and was handcuffed to a nearby tree where he continued to scream his innocence. Booth had already decided to die rather than give himself up.

Lieutenant Doherty was in charge of the party and he made his mind up to take immediate action. "Smoking out" his quarry seemed the least risky and quickest way to bring the siege to an end. He gave orders for a rope of straw to be made. This was duly set on fire and thrown inside the barn, where it landed on a pile of straw. The straw caught fire and began to burn ferociously, which forced Booth toward the door. The soldiers were under strict orders to bring Booth back alive to face justice, but

Sergeant Boston Corbett had Booth in his sights and fired his carbine. The bullet struck Booth in the back of the head, in almost the exact place that Lincoln had been hit. He fell and was quickly dragged outside by some soldiers. After lying there for a little while he whispered into the ear of an officer, "Tell my mother I died for my country and I did what I thought was best."

Booth's arms had been paralyzed from the effect of the bullet wound and he asked for his hands to be lifted so that he could see them for the last time. Looking at them, he said, "Useless. Useless." They were his final words.

Two and a half hours after he had been shot, just as the morning sun was rising and the cocks began to crow, John Wilkes Booth died.

Booth had conspired with several others in the assassination. Eight were sent to trial, and four of them were executed by hanging, including Mary Surratt, Booth's landlady.

There was a mighty outpouring of grief across the nation for the death of Abraham Lincoln. He had twelve funerals, each more lavish than the previous one, as the train which carried his body from Washington to his home in Illinois crossed the country. The cortege stopped from town to town, first in Baltimore, then through Philadelphia and New York. Immense crowds marched alongside each funeral procession; in New York it was estimated that 75,000 marched, as well as 11,000 military. In Albany, on the day of Lincoln's funeral in the town, the news came through that John Wilkes Booth had been tracked down and killed.

There was no funeral for the assassin.

LEE HARVEY OSWALD

Lee Harvey Oswald (1939–1963) shot and assassinated U.S. president John Fitzgerald Kennedy (1917–1963) in Dallas, Texas. He was himself shot and killed two days later by Jack Ruby in full view of the press photographers and news film cameramen. The film footage of both deaths has been viewed in minute detail countless times around the world since that day.

Oswald had joined the U.S. Marine Corps at age seventeen, but in 1959 he defected to the Soviet Union. He returned in 1962 and achieved early notoriety in the press for this unusual reverse defection.

Despite rumors that he had been part of an assassination conspiracy, in 1964 the Warren Commission decided that Oswald had acted single-handedly. In contrast, the 1979 House Select Committee on Assassinations concluded that Oswald was "probably part of a conspiracy."

JAMES EARL RAY

James Earl Ray (1928–1998) was an escaped prisoner who was convicted of the assassination of Dr. Martin Luther King Jr. (1929–1968) in Memphis, Tennessee.

There are conflicting views about Ray's guilt. The King family itself has cast doubt on this. Although Ray pled guilty before trial, some think it was only a plea bargain to avoid execution. Ray escaped from prison but was recaptured after only three days. He died in prison from complications related to kidney disease.

PATTY HEARST

Patricia Campbell Hearst (b. 1954) is the granddaughter of William Randolph Hearst, the press baron and builder of San Simeon, California. Hers was a gilded childhood.

In 1974, Hearst was kidnapped by the Symbionese Liberation Army (SLA) and held for ransom. During her captivity she appeared to join her captors and embrace their cause. She was photographed taking part in a bank robbery, and the pictures of her during the robbery were shown around the world. She became a "cause celebre."

During her stay with the SLA she assumed the name "Tania," the same as Che Guevara's girlfriend-cum-comrade.

Hearst was arrested in 1975 and was put on trial the following year. Immediately following her capture, she had declared her affiliation to the SLA, but by the time of the trial she had changed her tune and claimed she had been tortured and abused in captivity. She also claimed she had been coerced into taking part in the robberies. She was found guilty and sentenced to seven years in prison, of which she served twenty-two months.

On the final day of his presidency, Bill Clinton signed a full pardon for Patty Hearst.

TIMOTHY McVEIGH

Timothy James McVeigh (1968–2001) was executed by lethal injection for the unlawful killing of 168 people in the Alfred P. Murrah

Building in Oklahoma City on April 19, 1995. At that time, the Oklahoma bombing was the deadliest act of terrorism in the history of the United States. Terrorism on home soil had not been a major factor in American life until this outrage, and it quickly dominated news stories, not only in the USA, but around the world. Only the destruction of the World Trade Center on September 11, 2001 caused more casualties.

McVeigh was a U.S. Army veteran who served in the First Gulf War. The explosive device he used to destroy the building was homemade and consisted of 5,000 pounds of ammonium nitrate and nitro-methane. He packed the explosives in a small truck and parked outside the building. After lighting the fuses, McVeigh ran away, and the blast was so powerful that he was lifted off his feet despite being over a block away when it exploded. Seventeen young children were killed in the day care center on the ground floor.

He claimed that his attack, which occurred on the second anniversary of the Waco Siege, was revenge against what he considered to be a "tyrannical government."

"A criminal is a person with predatory instincts who does not have sufficient capital to form a corporation."

—Howard Scott (1890–1970)

Masters of
Change

Several men and women have rocked the world as it revolved on its axis. Until well into the nineteenth century, the best ways to make changes of this size were either war or religion. Someone had to die or someone had to submit to a belief. There were no peaceful ways to change the world.

Julius Caesar changed the map of the known world by conquest, and Jesus of Nazareth began Christianity. They are the best known in the fields of war and religion, but many others have followed.

In the nineteenth century, the world dived into the Scientific Age. The freedom to conduct experiments allowed greater discoveries to be made. In this climate, a few people rose and changed the whole world.

Among the greatest were these Americans.

THOMAS ALVA EDISON (1847–1931)
Electricity

Edison was the first to bring in cheap electricity to serve industry and the home. Once the supplies had been established, electricity brought light to the dark streets, it powered machines to save labor, and it lit homes at the touch of a switch.

Edison also led new developments in the field of sound reproduction (phonograph) and the way film is shown (kinetoscope).

ALEXANDER GRAHAM BELL (1847–1922)
Telephone

Bell invented the telephone and changed the way people communicated with each other. No longer were they hostage to the postal system or the telegraph, but suddenly they were able to speak directly across vast distances.

PHILO T. FARNSWORTH (1906–1971)
Television

Farnsworth brought in the television age with his all-electronic means of transmitting pictures. Until Farnsworth, the idea of transmitting pictures electronically was no more than a science fiction dream.

JOHN F. KENNEDY (1917–1963)
The Moon

U.S. president John F. Kennedy made sure the human race kept its focus on the big picture. In 1961, in a speech to a Joint Session of Congress, Kennedy said, "First I believe this nation should commit itself to achieving the goal, before this decade is out, of landing a man on the Moon and returning him safely to the Earth." People listened, but few were convinced; after all, the Soviets were well ahead in the race.

Then in 1962, the full megawattage of Kennedy's blazing rhetoric was seen and heard in one of the greatest speeches of his short life. In it he spoke the famous words, "We choose to go to the Moon in this decade and do the other things, not because they are easy, but because they are hard."

If ever there was a "call to arms" for a national and international peaceful endeavor, this was it. Men did land on the Moon and return safely within the decade. Little more than a year after his speech, JFK lay dead, the victim of an assassin's bullet. He never got to see the fruits of his legacy.

And another thing . . .

In 1954–1955, while he was recovering from an operation on his spine, Kennedy wrote *Profiles in Courage*, a book that describes eight examples of senators who risked their careers to stand up for their personal beliefs. He was awarded the 1957 Pulitzer Prize for Biography and remains the only U.S. president to be so honored.

MARTIN LUTHER KING (1929–1968)
Antiracialist

Mention his name, and people think of his great speeches, his philosophy of passive resistance, and his assassination. King's legacy is not yet fully realized, but he lit the torch for racial harmony.

Martin Luther King's preeminence among the greatest orators of the twentieth century touched the hearts and souls of all but those who would not listen. He had the rare ability to change the minds of the people who listened to him, and he was able to convince them of the wisdom of his words.

MARGARET SANGER (1879–1966)
Contraception

The three major figures in the development of the oral contraceptive are Margaret Sanger (1879–1966), who, in her eighties, raised the initial $150,000 to fund the oral contraceptive research project; Frank Colton (1923–2003), who invented Enovid, the first oral contraceptive); and Carl Djerassi (b. 1923), who developed the modern "pill."

Margaret Sanger, an Irish American from a poor working-class family in New York, is widely regarded as the founder of the birth-control movement in the USA. She opened a birth-control clinic in 1916 in New York and published *What Every Girl Should Know*, which provided basic information about topics such as menstruation and sexual feelings. Police were alerted and raided the clinic. Sanger, who had been mailing out birth-control advice, was arrested for distributing obscene material by post, contrary to U.S. Post Office regulations. To escape prosecution Sanger left the USA to live in Europe. She returned in 1917, published *What Every Mother Should Know*, and was promptly rearrested and sent to the workhouse for "creating a public nuisance."

> "I was resolved to seek out the root of the evil, to do something to change the destiny of mothers whose miseries were as vast as the sky."
> **—Margaret Sanger, 1931**

The pill, as the oral contraceptive is widely known, was introduced to the public in 1961. Women were finally able to take necessary precautions themselves, and no longer had to rely on men. The enhanced sensations of condom-free sex and the combined feelings of emancipation from the straitlaced late 1940s and 1950s ushered in the freedoms of what is known as the "sexual revolution."

THOMAS NAST (1840–1902)
Santa Claus

A small indulgence, but here is my favorite master of change:
Thomas Nast is almost unknown outside of America, but his dramatic, illustrative skill with paintbrushes helped to change the course

of American history, and therefore, the world. He also sketched a little brightness into the lives of millions of children around the world.

Nast was massively influential in a way that modern caricaturists can only dream of. His cartoons were published in *Harper's Weekly*, which was a widely read and politically influential magazine in the late nineteenth century. Nash's cartoons have been credited as a vital help in electing four United States presidents.

Abraham Lincoln (1809–1865) commented that Nast was his best recruiting sergeant. He was a fierce Unionist and in a melodramatic cartoon in *Harper's Weekly*, which was given the prominence of a double spread about twenty inches wide, Nast portrayed a Union amputee shaking the hand of a neatly dressed Southern soldier. The figure of Columbia stood weeping at the grave of Union soldiers. The picture was titled *Compromise with the South*.

This widely circulated image was said to have gotten Lincoln reelected in 1864.

During the presidential race of 1872, Nast savaged the candidacy of Horace Greeley (1811–1872) the editor of the *New York Tribune*. In one cartoon he was shown murdering African Americans. Nast's work paved the way for the election of Ulysses Grant (1822–1885).

In 1876, Nast played an important part in the election of Rutherford Hayes (1822–1893). After the election, Hayes stated that Nast was the single most powerful aid he had, but soon Nast began to oppose Hayes's policies. Hayes was fortunate that Nast was denied the same level of access as before at *Harper's*, which restricted his ability to attack.

In the 1884 presidential race, Nast championed Grover Cleveland (1837–1908). Nast—though he had been a Republican all his life— harbored a distrust of James Blaine, the Republican candidate. His support of Cleveland was conceded at the time to have won him the small margin that made all the difference.

Most importantly, Thomas Nast also changed the way children of the world perceive Santa Claus. He was the first to draw Santa as a jolly, rotund figure in a red coat. Until Nast's famous drawings, Santa had been portrayed as a tall, thin, somewhat imposing figure. In the pre–Nast era, Santa looked as if he was reluctantly parting with a small charitable donation, and probably doling out some cautionary advice to go along with it. Nast's Santa was different. He looked like everybody's favorite uncle, embracing everyone and dishing out presents to the kids at Christmas. Nast had managed to add, in a few strokes of his magical brush, a little joy to the lives of children everywhere.

So—not bad for a mere cartoonist—a pivotal involvement in the election of four U.S. presidents, and bringing Santa Claus alive in the eyes of the world's children.

In 1902 Nast was appointed U.S. Consul General to Ecuador and later that year he died there in a yellow fever outbreak. He had stayed behind to make sure all U.S. personnel were safe from the disease, but tragically, he himself succumbed.

Sayings

BORN IN THE USA

American sayings have a way of traveling around the world. It probably has something to do with Hollywood films and American TV shows, both of which are seen in most countries.

In the post–World War II years, most countries labored under dour conditions. America looked like the only beacon of hope and excitement around. Those who lived in other countries all wanted a bit of America and the bit they took was the way Americans spoke. They couldn't all go to the States, but they could certainly sound as if they'd been there.

Everyday expressions such as *french fries* instead of *chips* and *eggs over easy* for a simple *fried egg*, have crept into common usage in other English- speaking countries. In England, the use of *truck* instead of *lorry* is starting to take hold.

Other lesser-known expressions such as *Va Va Voom!* have spread into Latin America and some European countries.

American sayings tend to be more expressive and descriptive than those found in standard English. Here are a few.

YUPPIE

Yuppie is short for "young, urban professional" or "young, upwardly mobile professional."

The short-story writer Joseph Epstein (b. 1937) is sometimes credited with the first written use of the word in 1982, although there is a single earlier reference in 1980. The term "yuppie" gained currency during the 1980s, but was used less after the stock market crash of 1987, when a significant number of yuppies found themselves jobless.

Yuppie and other amusing derivatives such as "DINK" (double income no kids) remain in use around the world.

COOL

To be "cool" is to be accepted—to have status.

Cool is constantly changing. It signifies composure and self-control and it can be used as an expression of approval. The most notable use of cool began with African American vernacular English and its close connection with jazz music. The theory exists that jazz clubs became hotter as the night's music played on into the early hours, and the way for owners to reduce the stifling atmosphere was to open the doors and windows, and restore the "cool." The slow late-night music played in those scenes came to be associated with the opening of the windows, and it was called "cool."

The modern notion of being cool and the associated "chill" and "chill out" also originated in African American culture, and have successfully migrated around the world.

OK (OKAY)

OK is by far the most recognized word or expression in the world. It is used in the languages of most countries, including almost all Arab countries, Latin America, and Europe. Even Far Eastern countries like Japan and Taiwan have adopted OK into common parlance.

There are several different versions of the origin of OK. One version has it that *okeh* was originally used by Native Americans (Choctaw) to signify "it is so," and was adopted into American English by the settlers.

Other versions include the Greek "Ola Kala," meaning all correct, but the American lexicographer Allen Walker Read (1906–2002) made a special study of OK, and concluded that "Oll Korrect" was the full spelling. This derived from the early nineteenth-century fad for deliberate comic misspelling of expressions, and then abbreviating them for additional comic effect. Newspaper records of the time lend weight to this view.

The simple expedient of saying "OK" can imply approval, give sanction or authorization, and confirm that something is all right, or conversely, no more than mediocre. OK is also used as an exclamation, to draw the attention of other people ("OK—stop what you're doing.")

"OK" is universally understood, and can be used in almost any part of speech—noun, verb, or adjective. Most importantly computer modal dialogue boxes use an OK button to receive the command to proceed.

HIYA

This is a shortened form of "How are you?" Now it's even shorter as the ubiquitous "Hi!" has taken hold. The most used salutation in e-mails is "Hi," almost as if to signify that the sender is young at heart and "switched on" enough to know how to speak e-mail.

VA VA VOOM!

Va Va Voom! is an expression that has no literal meaning, but is meant to convey that the speaker is ecstatically happy about something—generally the thing about which they have just finished speaking.

1974 Oscar winner Art Carney (1918–2003) was the first to use the expression "Va Va Va Voom" (notice the extra "Va") in a song in the 1950s. It has been shortened in the intervening half century.

YA KNOW WHAT I MEAN?

An expression often tacked on to the end of a declamatory sentence, to double-check that the listener has understood the intended meaning.

From 1948 to 1950 Art Carney played the doorman on *The Morey Amsterdam Show* on radio and television. His catchphrase was "Ya know what I mean?" It is still in common usage on both sides of the Atlantic more than fifty years after the show ended.

SKID ROW

A person who is down on their luck, or bankrupt, or heading for a life with no prospects, is said to be "on skid row."

In U.S. logging towns, timber was often moved around by being skidded down a hill or a corduroy road.

In Seattle, one of these streets was actually called Skid Road and it became the haunt of people down on their luck. The name and its meaning have morphed into the modern term.

KICK ASS

To enforce one's will on another—maybe by violent means.

Immortalized by General Norman Schwartzkopf in the First Gulf War in a pre-attack press briefing. One of the attending foreign journalists asked what the plan for the next day was and Sir Peter de la Billiere, leading the British troops, went into a long and detailed battle plan that had most of scribes nodding off.

When it came to Stormin' Norman's turn to set out his battle plan, he stepped up to the mike and said, "We're going to go in there and kick ass. We're going to kick ass. We're going to kick ass."

It was a striking lesson on the effectiveness of simple, direct, and descriptive language.

Next day Schwarzkopf and his troops kicked ass.

"When placed in command—take charge."
—Norman Schwartzkopf (b. 1934)

Weapons of War

I n the defense of the nation, the United States of America has seen the invention of some of the most lethal weapons ever devised by man.

> "Jaw jaw is better than war war."
>
> **—Winston Churchill**

REVOLVER

Connecticut-born Samuel Colt (1814–1862) developed the revolver. Legend has it that Colt, who was working as a deckhand on a ship, observed the way the capstan worked to lift the anchor, and formed the idea of a self-loading firearm.

The unique feature of Colt's design was that six rounds of ammunition were held ready in a cylindrical revolving magazine, each round to be fired through a single barrel. Previous attempts at automatic loading had involved the use of revolving barrels and a single loading mechanism. The Colt design saved both cost and weight, and was far more reliable. Colt patented his idea in England and France in 1835 and in the USA in 1836.

The production line and interchangeable parts were developed by Colt with the help of Eli Whitney (1765–1825) in order to produce the vast number of revolvers needed by the U.S. Army in the 1845–1848 war with Mexico.

GATLING GUN

In 1861, the Gatling Gun was put to use for the first time as a weapon in the American Civil War.

Dr. Richard Gatling (1818–1903) developed the world's first successful machine gun. It was hand-cranked with multiple barrels and used cartridges that contained the primer, propellant, and bullet. It was capable of firing 200 rounds per minute.

Gatling believed his gun was so powerful that it would bring all war to an end. He felt that armies would consider it unthinkable to ask their soldiers to face the carnage his gun was capable of dealing out.

MAXIM GUN

In 1884, Hiram Maxim (1840–1916), born in Sangerville, Maine, invented the first truly automatic machine gun. Previous machine guns had to use hand-cranking or even electric power to create the continuous firing, but the Maxim Gun used some of the escaping explosive gases (from the cartridge) and the recoil force to eject the spent cartridge from the breech and load the next one. It could fire 600 rounds per minute.

As the gun only had a single barrel and a smaller firing mechanism, it was far lighter than the Gatling Gun, which made it portable.

Maxim also invented an electric lightbulb, but in 1881, when it became clear that Edison had a better product and controlled the American market, he emigrated to England.

In 1909, Maxim invented the gun silencer, which he called "The Suppressor."

> "Whatever happens we have got The Maxim Gun and they have not."
>
> **—Hilaire Belloc** (1970–1953),
> writing at the start of World War I.

SUBMARINE

The first submarine to be used in war was the *Turtle*. In 1776, David Bushnell (1742–1824), a student at Yale University, designed the *Turtle*, which was built by the U.S. Navy to his specification, using a screw propeller. Sergeant Ezra Lee sailed it close to a British battleship in New York Harbor, planning to attach explosives to the hull by drilling into it. The hull of the British ship turned out to be too tough and the attempt failed, but this was the first time a submarine had been used in war.

The first submarine to deliver and detonate a torpedo successfully was the Confederate CSS *H.L. Hunley*, in 1864 during the American Civil War. The torpedo, which had been attached to the bow of the *Hunley*, sank its target, the USS *Housatonic*. Unfortunately for the crew, the captain of the Hunley left its hatch open during the action and the vessel was swamped by the wave from the explosion. It sank with the loss of all on board.

In 2000, the *Hunley* was raised from the seabed, and it is now in the process of restoration.

The modern torpedo guidance system was invented in 1942 by the great Hollywood beauty Hedy Lamarr (1914–2000). At the time, torpedoes had the alarming habit, if they missed their primary target, of circling round and blowing up the submarine that fired them. Lamarr patented the invention, which was based on frequency switching, but the patent ran out before it was taken up by the military.

Simon Lake aboard his submarine Argonaut Junior

Other major advances in submarine development came from one of America's most prolific inventors, Simon Lake (1866–1945). Lake is almost unknown outside the United States, but he succeeded in patenting more than 200 inventions. He observed that one of the disadvantages of underwater travel was the inability to see what was happening on the surface. After applying his mind to the problem he came up with the first version of the modern periscope, which he called the "omniscope." This device used prisms and lenses in a complex array to allow the underwater observer to see forwards. He modified this later to make all-round vision possible.

Lake designed two of the more bizarre underwater vessels ever built: the *Argonaut* and the *Argonaut Junior* (which was made of wood). Both were equipped with wheels to allow them to crawl along the bottom of shallow seas or riverbeds, and had airlocks to allow divers to enter and depart during submersion.

And another thing . . .

Lake's uncle, Jesse, invented the "caterpillar" tractor.

STEALTH

Certain shapes show up more easily on radar screens. Stealth technology employs radical changes to the designs of both airframes and engines that enable aircraft to fly missions into highly defended target areas, with no loss of capability, and yet avoid being detected by radar.

The first aircraft to employ stealth capability was the U.S. F-117A Nighthawk. The Nighthawk—originally code-named Senior Trend—had its first test flight in 1981. The F-117A is produced by Lockheed Aeronautical Systems Co., and the first combat-ready aircraft was delivered to the U.S. Air Force in August 1982.

U.S. Air Combat Command's 4450th Tactical Group, the only F-117A unit, achieved operational capability in October 1983. The F-117A remained classified until 1988, and was first revealed to the public in 1990.

NUCLEAR WEAPONS

"The energy produced by the breaking down of the atom is a very poor kind of thing. Anyone who expects a source of power from the transformation of these atoms is talking moonshine."

—Ernest Rutherford (1871–1937), the first man to split the atom

Atomic fission was discovered in 1938 at the Kaiser Wilhelm Institute in Berlin by German chemist Otto Hahn (1879–1960) in cooperation with Dr. Fritz Strassman (1902–1980), a radio chemist.

The first detonation of an atomic bomb, known as the Trinity Test, took place on July 16, 1945, in the desert of New Mexico. The test was a spectacular success, and eyewitnesses from twenty miles away reported feeling the heat of the explosion.

The first atomic bomb detonated in war was dropped on Hiroshima on the mainland of Japan on August 6, 1945. Ninety percent of the city was destroyed. Out of a population of around 250,000 people, about 45,000 died on the first day, with a further 19,000 dying in the next four months.

On July 25, 1945, president Harry Truman (1884–1972) issued the bombing order to the Commander of U.S. Strategic Air Forces in the Pacific, General Carl "Tooey" Spaatz (1891–1974). Truman noted in his diary that he had ordered the bomb to be dropped on a "purely military target."

The Soviet Union was able to develop its first atom bomb in 1949 following the betrayal of U.S. nuclear secrets by the spy Klaus Fuchs (1911–1988). Fuchs was born in Germany and fled to England in the 1930s when the Gestapo began to round up communists. He worked on the British atomic-bomb research project before being transferred to the USA to work on the Manhattan Project. The Manhattan Project led to the development of the first atomic bomb. After his arrest for spying in 1949, and his trial in 1950, Fuchs was sentenced to fourteen years in prison, of which he served nine. On his release, Fuchs illegally relocated to East Germany, one of the Soviet vassal states, where he began lecturing in physics.

The world's first hydrogen bomb was detonated by the USA on November 1, 1952. The explosion of the device, which was code-named "Mike," caused the island of Elugelab in the Pacific to disappear. It left a crater 1 mile (1.6 kilometers) wide and 160 feet (48 meters) deep, and in the process 80 million tons of earth were lifted into the air. The characteristic mushroom cloud rose to 57,000 feet in 90 seconds, and eventually spread to a width of 1,000 miles.

The results so terrified Norris Bradbury (1909–1997), the director of Los Alamos, the US National Laboratory, that he considered keeping the magnitude of the detonation secret.

The bomb resulted from a meeting in 1949 between President Truman and Edward Teller (1908–2003), known as the father of the hydrogen bomb, who pressed for an urgent study to be undertaken for the development of a superbomb. The plan was to build a thermonuclear device, which ultimately came to be known as the hydrogen bomb. Truman authorized a crash development program, which drew immediate opposition from many, including Robert Oppenheimer (1904–1967), who had led the team which developed the first atom bomb in 1945.

The Soviets' first true hydrogen (fusion) bomb was detonated on November 22, 1955. Within the Soviet Union, it was named "Sakharov's Third Idea," having been designed by the famous scientist (and later dissident), Andre Sakharov (1921–1989).

The first submarine-launched nuclear missile, known as Polaris, was deployed by the U.S. Navy. It was test launched on July 20, 1960, the first-ever underwater rocket launch.

Last Words

Bruce Springsteen's immortal song, "Born in the U.S.A.," was a great patriotic blast expressing American pride (as well as sadness for the hardships faced by returning Vietnam veterans). It gave a voice to people who wanted to be heard.

If you've read this far and not just skipped to the end, you'll already appreciate why being "Born in the USA" is such a good thing. But how can a country that has only five percent of the world's population develop more civilizing "stuff" than the remaining ninety-five percent put together? Through the eyes of this outsider, it comes down to three important freedoms that are so easy to take for granted, but so hard-won:

- freedom of speech
- freedom of movement
- freedom of opportunity

It is self-evident to open-minded people that these freedoms release the talents of those who possess them. And it is difficult to understand why the stellar example set by the USA is not followed by more countries.

BORN IN THE USA

"'Freedom' is an indivisible word. If we want to enjoy it and fight for it, we must be prepared to extend it to everyone, whether they are rich or poor, whether they agree with us or not, no matter what their race or the color of their skin."

—Wendell Willkie (1892-1944)

(U.S. presidential candidate 1940)

In a Utopian society—which is a community of perfection—there is no poverty, no misery, and few laws.

No one would claim that the USA is Utopia.

Even America's closest friends in Britain and Europe view some elements of US life with deep reservation. The Ku Klux Klan, for example, is not something America can be proud of, and some of the most infamous criminals in history have been born in the USA. Surprisingly, considering it is the most medically advanced country on Earth, (the home of the artificial heart and the polio vaccine), there is no National Health Service in the USA, and it is difficult for the European mind to understand why this should be.

But against a small catalog of shortcomings, it has to be understood that America is a young country, and in its short history it has gone from a standing start to setting the pace for the rest of the world in science, literature, inventions, music, medicine, and many other fields. Its business leaders have created world-class companies that have conquered world markets and generated wealth for Americans and non-Americans alike. Its armies freed Europe twice in the twentieth century.

Almost within living memory, the lives of men and women were dominated by menial and unpalatable tasks. Collecting household dust was done with a brush and pan; houses were lit with candles or paraffin lamps; and writing to someone on the other side of the Earth could take three months. Enter: the vacuum cleaner, the lightbulb, the e-mail. More recently, it was only the dreams of science fiction writers to imagine holding a conversation with someone on the other side of the world while walking along a street. Enter: the cell phone.

These few, life-enriching products were developed by Americans, and there are hundreds if not thousands more where those came from.

To summarize, in the eyes of the world, America is the greatest hope for a stable and civilized world still left, and despite its troubles, it remains a country unmatched in the sum of its benefits, which is reason enough for wanting to be "Born in the USA."